Arching for Pleasure

A Collection of Erotic Foot Tales

by

Luna Wylde

Arching for Pleasure. A Collection of Erotic Foot Tales.

© 2024 by Luna Wylde

ISBN: 9798324286989

Imprint: Independently published

www.lunawylde.com

Here's to the fellas who are both under my spell and under my feet. You're the unsung heroes of my writing journey, doubling as my loyal fans and inadvertent footrests. Cheers to you!

Luna x

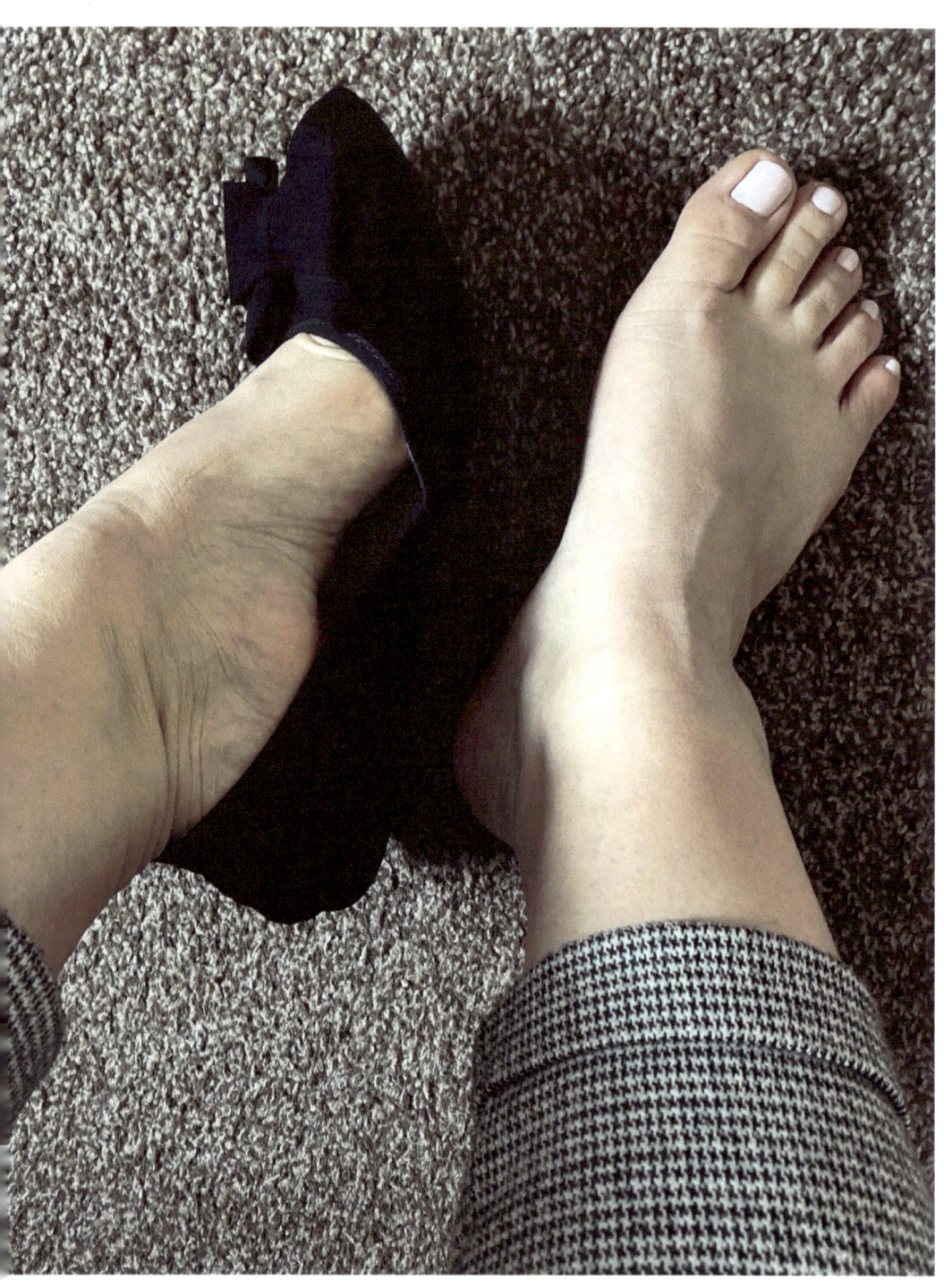

Footsteps of Desire.
A Diary of Unspoken Longings

As I walked through the door, the weight of the day seemed to settle on my shoulders, but it was my feet that bore the brunt of it all. The tightness and heat radiating from my shoes were like an echo of the day's trials. Dropping my bag with a sigh of relief, I carefully slid off my flat ballerina shoes, feeling each part release its grip on my tired feet. Ah, the sweet sensation of freedom.

With each step towards the living room, my toes wiggled in anticipation of the impending liberation. A glass of cold water beckoned to me, promising to quench not only my thirst but also the heat that had built up within my soles. Settling into the plush embrace of my sofa, I pulled a footstool closer, a silent invitation for my weary feet to rest.

Closing my eyes, I indulged in the simple pleasure of scrunching and stretching my feet, willing the tension to melt away with each movement. And then, unexpectedly, I felt it—a gentle touch, barely there yet undeniably present. Opening my eyes, I met your gaze, a mix of curiosity and hesitation playing across your features.

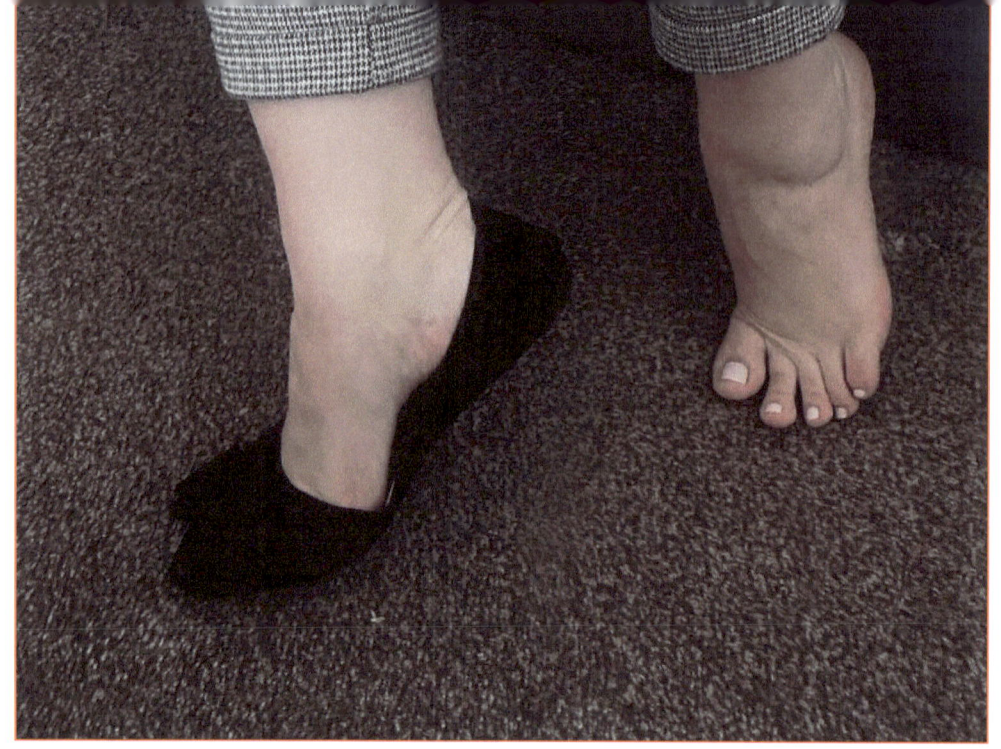

It wasn't a secret that you harboured a fascination with my feet, stealing glances whenever I dared to wear open-toed shoes or padded around the flat barefoot. But as my flatmate, you kept your desires hidden, buried beneath layers of polite conversation and friendly gestures. Yet, in that fleeting moment, I saw a glimpse of something more—a longing that mirrored my own secret fantasies.

In my mind's eye, I had often imagined you kneeling beside me, your warm hands enveloping my tired feet in a tender embrace. I could almost feel the rhythmic pressure of your fingers, easing away the knots and tension until all that remained was a blissful sense of surrender. It was a fantasy that filled my quiet moments, a whispered hope that perhaps one day our desires would align, and you would have the courage to make your intentions known.

But for now, we remained trapped in the silence of unspoken desires, each longing for something more yet hesitant to take that first step towards fulfilment. And so, with a bittersweet smile, I returned to the simple pleasure of scrunching my feet, knowing that even in the absence of words, our shared desires lingered in the air like a promise waiting to be fulfilled.

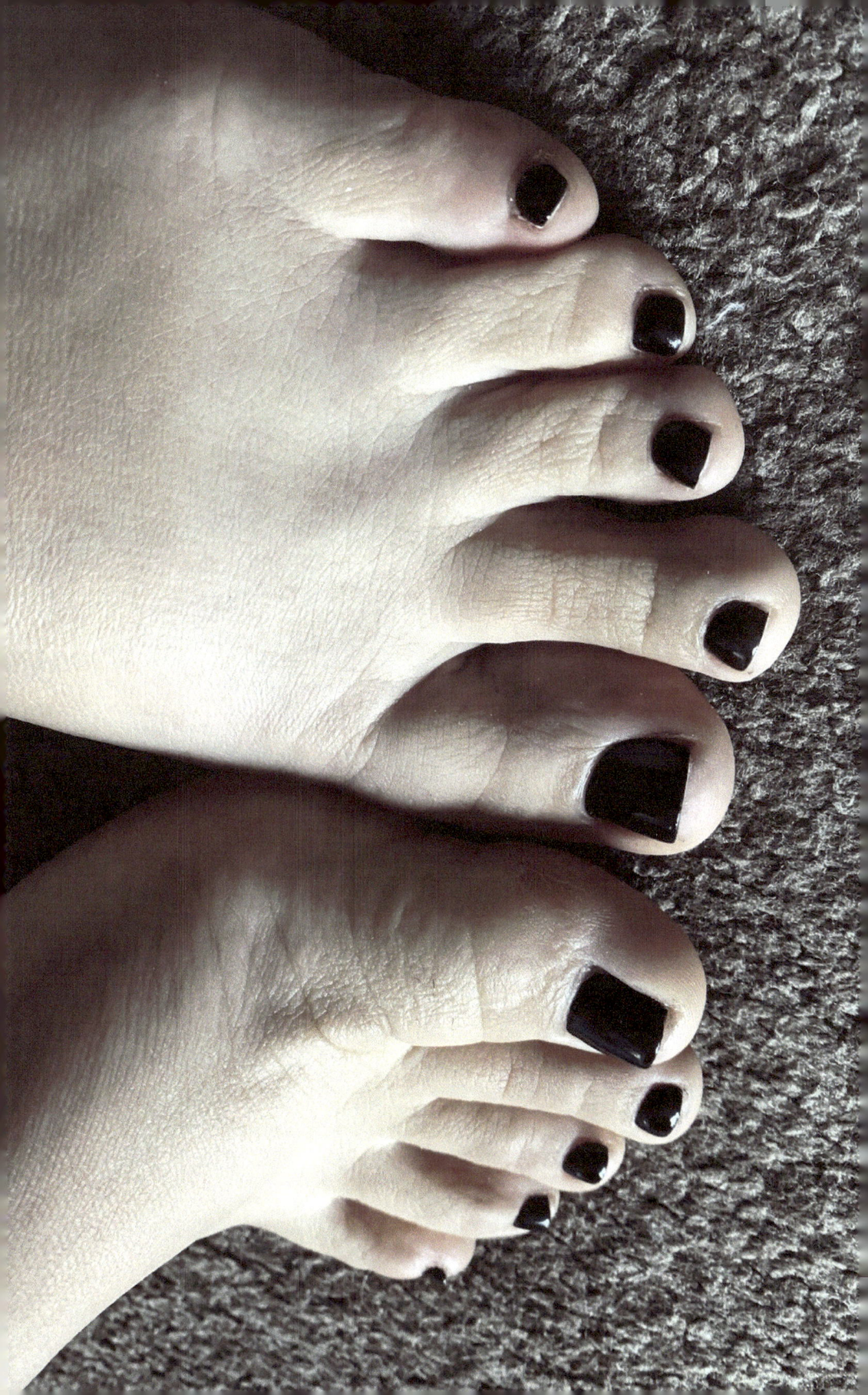

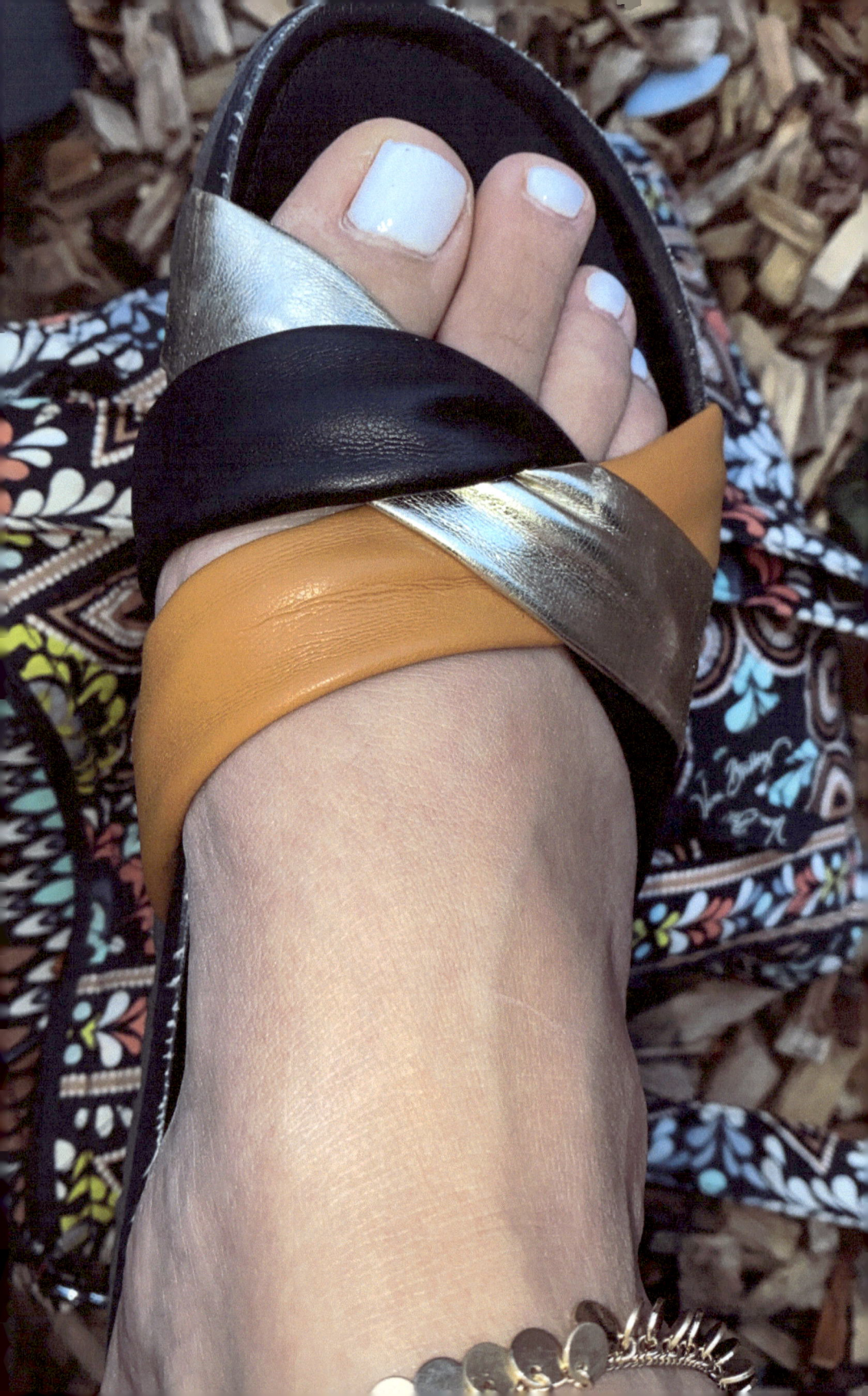

Summer Seduction:
A Sultry Soles Story of Obsession and Desire

In the sultry heat of summer, I found myself entangled in a little game of seduction with a guy working in the local shop. Every day, I made sure to look my absolute best, but not in the usual way. It wasn't about the clothes or the makeup for me—it was all about what lay below my knees.

This guy, he had a thing for feet, a real obsession. I noticed how he would stare longingly at other women's feet, and I couldn't resist the urge to capture that attention for myself. I wanted him to be completely enthralled by me, to the point where he couldn't think of anyone else.

So, every day, I made my way past the shop, wearing sandals that showcased my delicate arches, open-toe heels that hinted at the painted perfection of my toenails, and anklets that jingled with every step. My skin was always soft and supple, my toenails adorned with colours to match my mood—white, black, pink, or fiery red.

And it worked like magic. I watched as he struggled to tear his gaze away from my feet, his blush betraying his inner turmoil. With each passing day, his resistance crumbled a little more until, after four weeks of tantalising torment, he finally asked me out.

He suggested a casual date at a nearby cafe, but I had a secret—one that filled me with a delicious anticipation. All the attention I had been lavishing on my feet had awakened a primal hunger within me, a desire that could only be satisfied by his adoration.

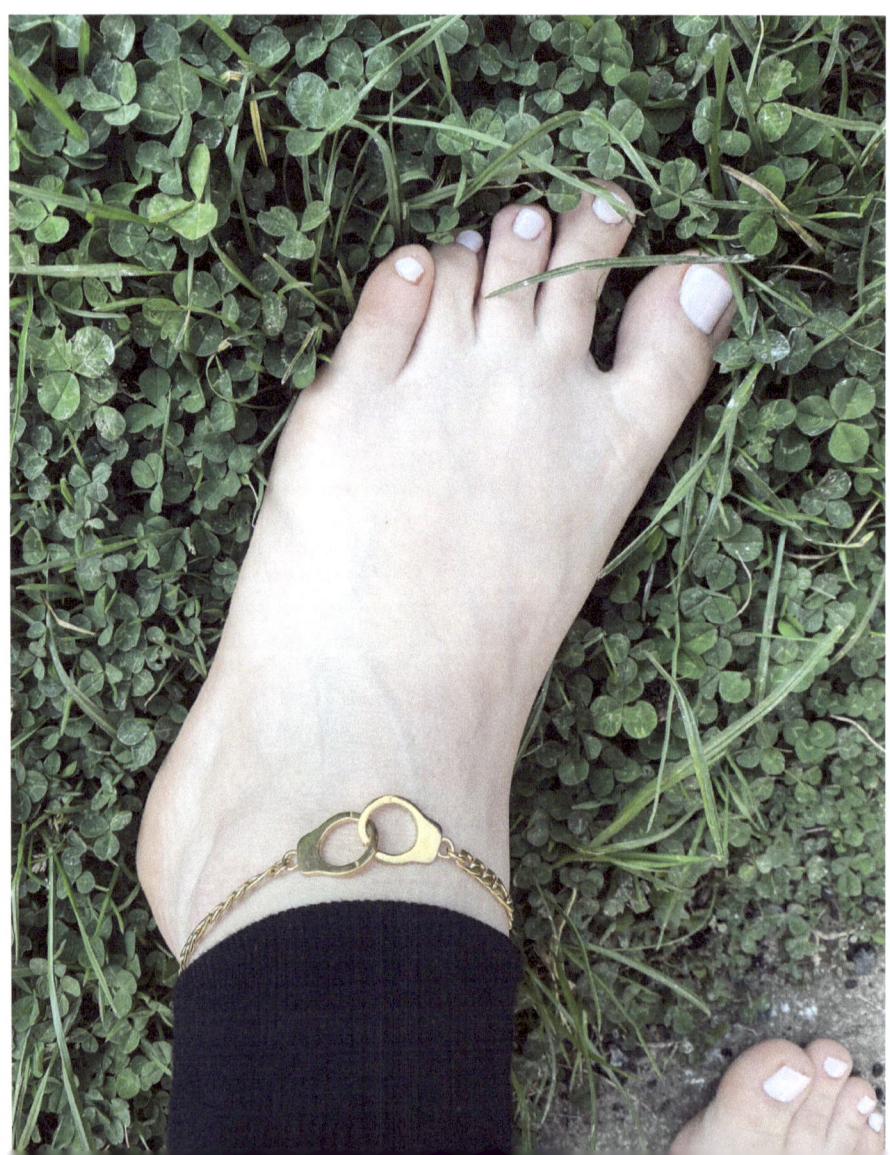

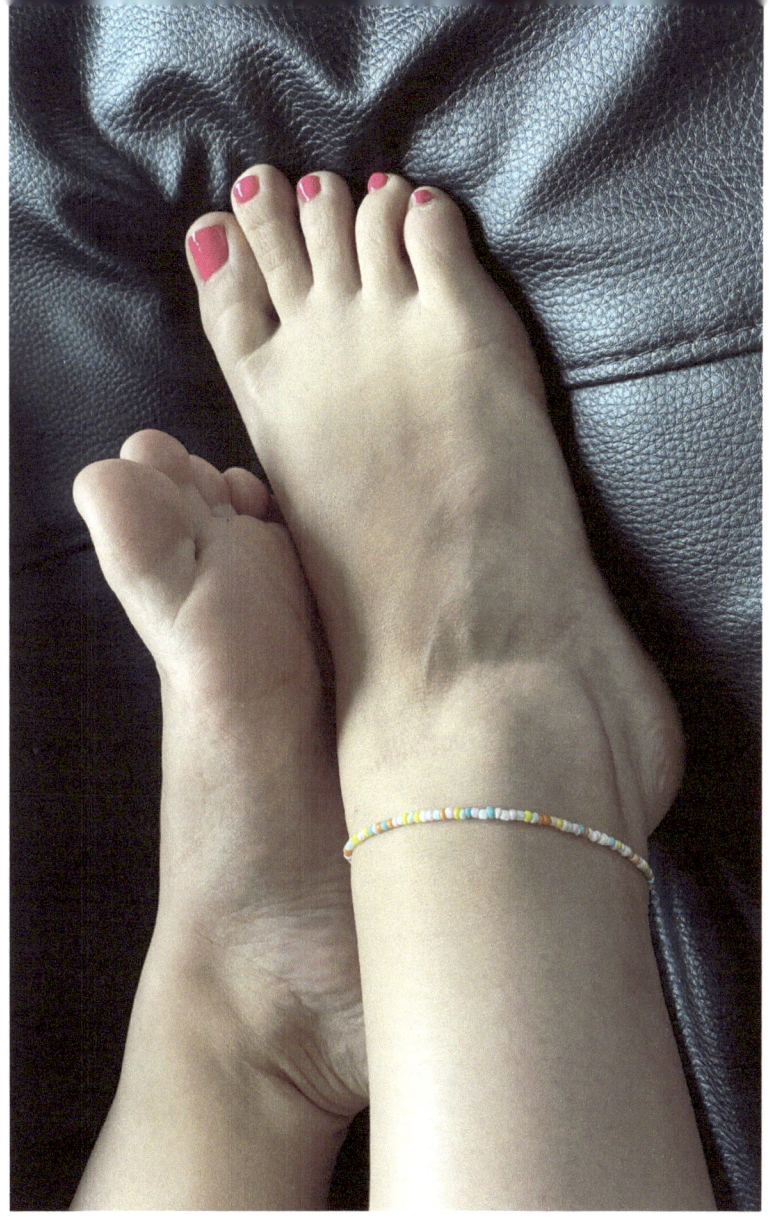

So, when he mumbled his invitation, I leaned in closer, meeting his gaze with a smouldering intensity. "How about we go to your place," I whispered, my voice low and husky with desire, "so you can show me just how much you love my feet?"

His eyes widened in surprise, but I could see the flicker of anticipation behind his shock. Without a word, he nodded, his resolve crumbling beneath the weight of my proposition.

And so, the stage was set for our sultry rendezvous—a night filled with the tantalising allure of feet. As we sat together in his apartment, he knelt before me, his hands reaching out to caress my feet with gentle reverence.

With each touch, I felt a wave of pleasure wash over me, my senses tingling with delight. His lips followed the path of his fingers, pressing soft kisses against the tender flesh of my feet. It was a dance of seduction unlike any other, a shared obsession that bound us together in a symphony of desire.

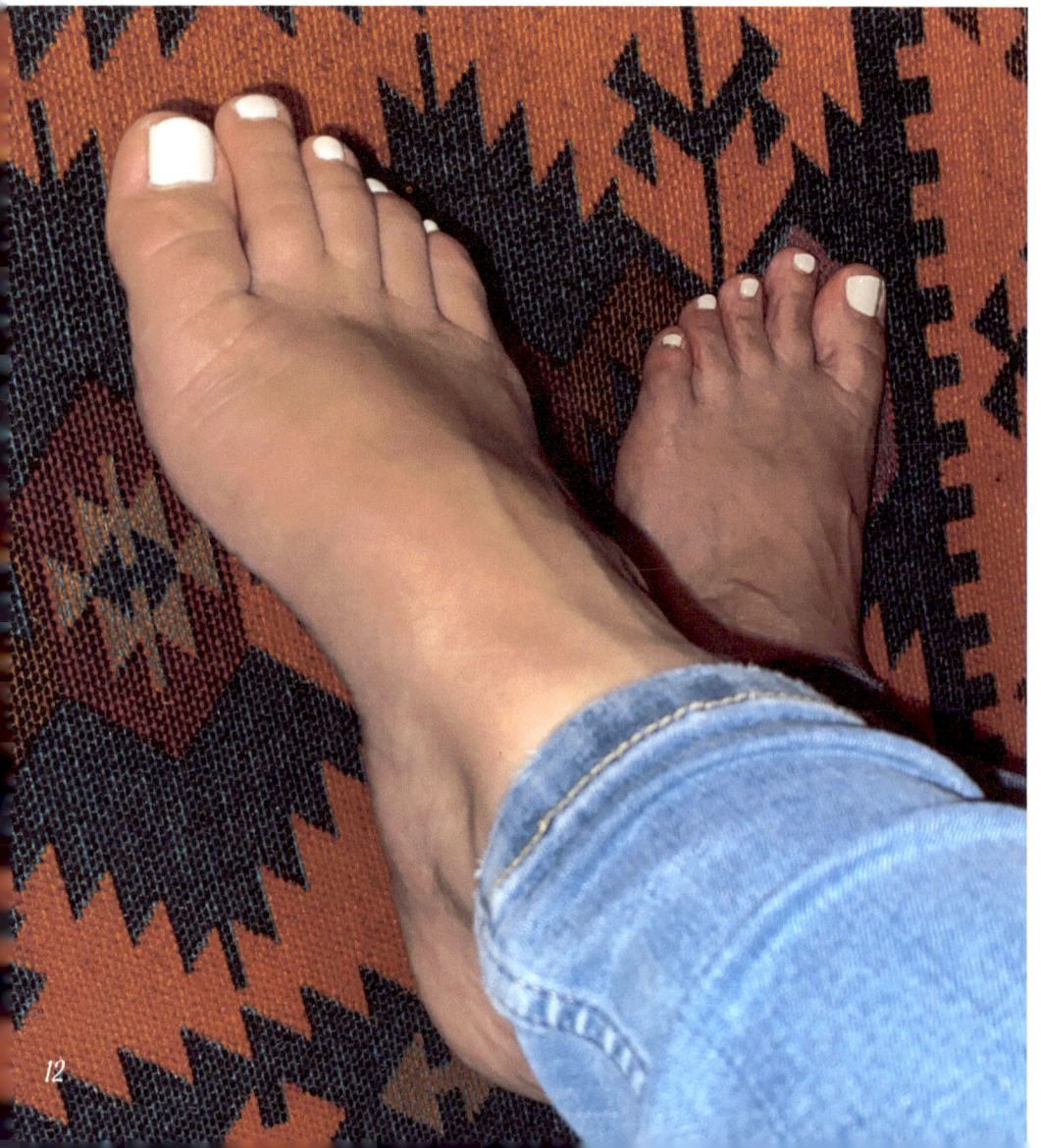

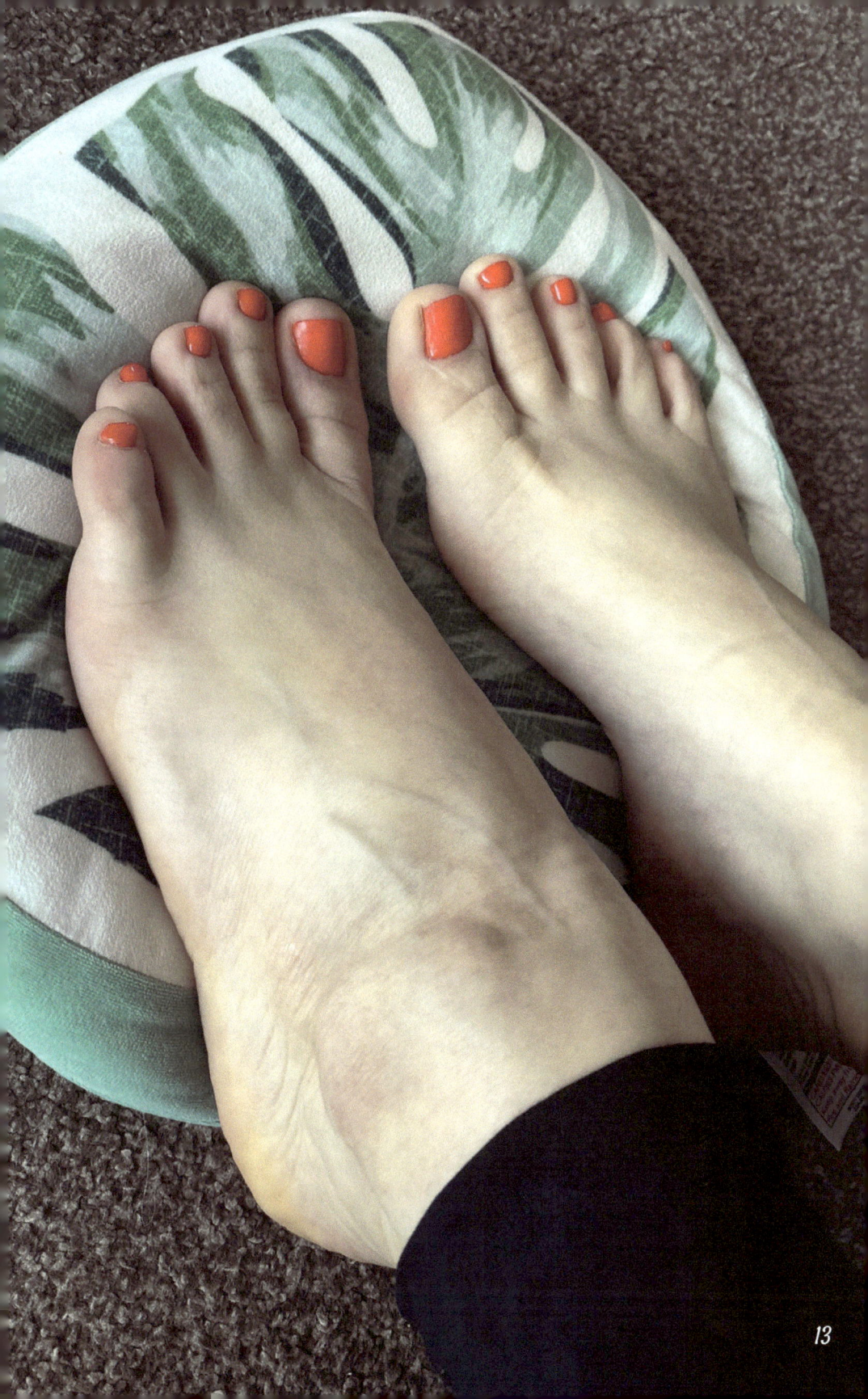

Sole Seduction

In the bustling aisles of the local grocery store, the air was heavy with the scent of fresh produce and the murmur of mundane conversations. Among the shoppers, there was one woman who commanded attention effortlessly. Her name was Stella, a woman in her mid-thirties, adorned in confidence and allure. She strutted down the aisles with purpose, her heels clicking against the linoleum floor.

Stella was a vision of confidence, her attire revealing just enough to captivate attention without giving away too much. But it wasn't just her attire that turned heads; it was her demeanour—fierce, independent, and unapologetically herself. And she had a particular penchant for shoes, especially the kind that accentuated her slender ankles and polished toenails.

Across the store, another figure stood out amidst the mundane backdrop. Adam, a successful man in his forties, exuded power and authority in his tailored suit. Yet, beneath his polished exterior lay a vulnerability—a weakness for confident women that left him feeling submissive and oddly fulfilled.

As Stella browsed the aisles, she noticed Adam discreetly stealing glances at her feet, clad in delicate, thin-strapped flip-flop sandals. A smirk played at the corners of her lips as she caught him in the act.

"You've got some nerve, you know that?" Stella's voice cut through the ambient noise, causing Adam to freeze in his tracks.

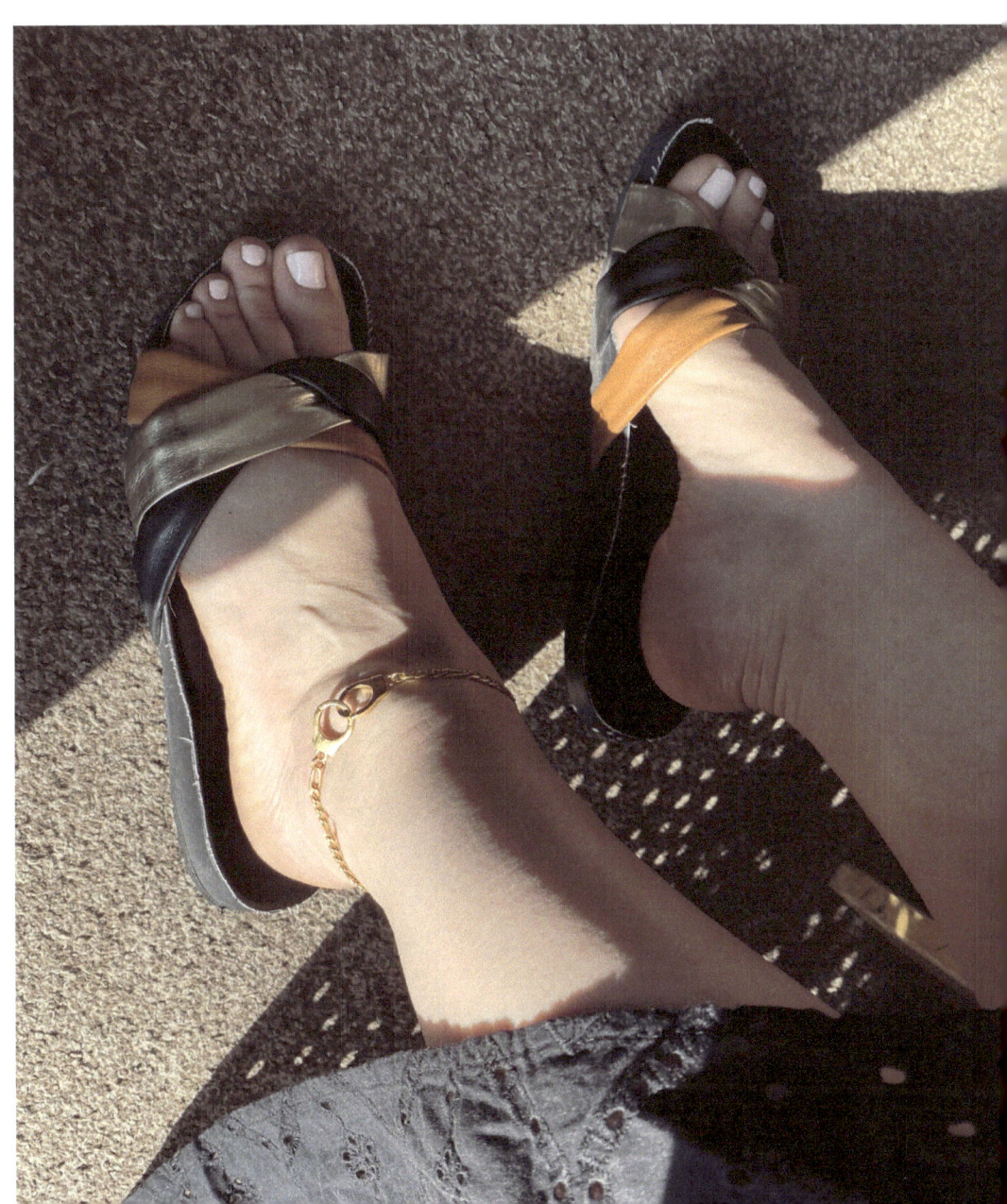

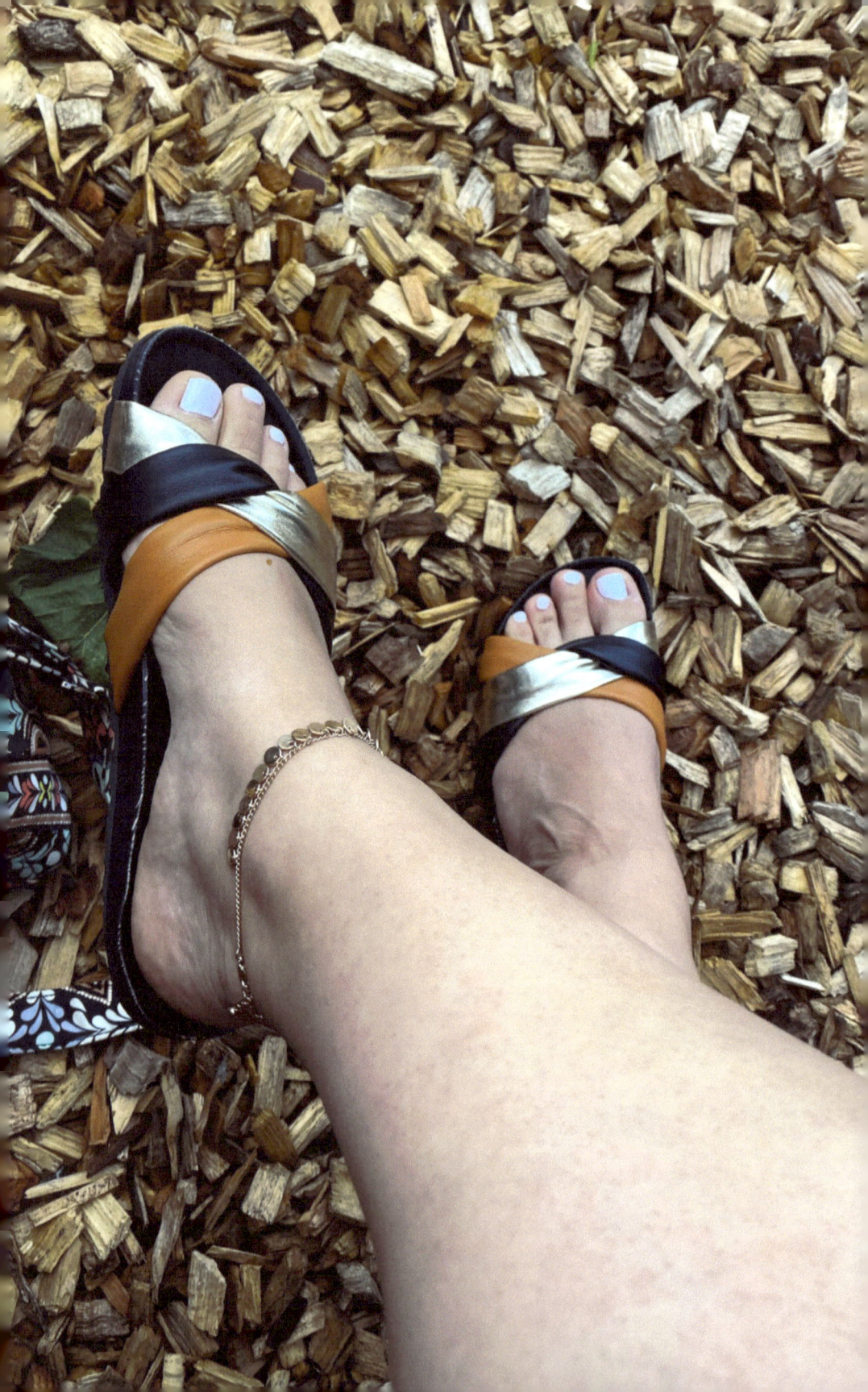

Adam's heart raced as he looked up, meeting Stella's gaze. He felt a flush of embarrassment creeping up his neck, his usual confidence crumbling in the presence of such a strong woman.

Stella continued, her voice dripping with disdain, "Creeping on a lady's feet in public? You must be desperate—or just a pathetic loser."

Adam's cheeks burned with shame, but beneath the humiliation, there was an inexplicable thrill. He found himself drawn to Stella's dominance, craving the humiliation she bestowed upon him.

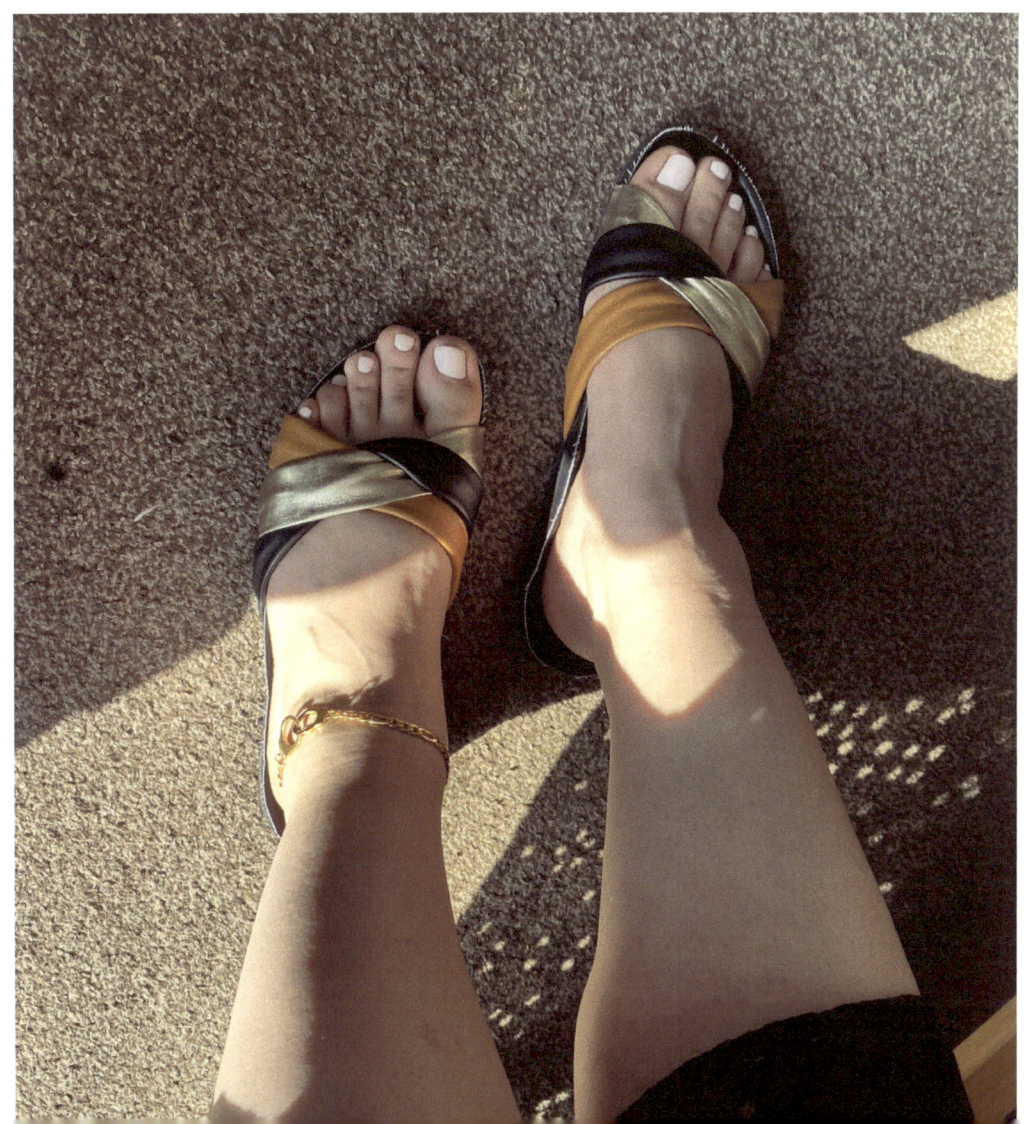

With a flick of her hair, Stella turned on her heel, her demeanour commanding Adam to follow. Without a word, he trailed behind her, his mind racing with a mixture of shame and excitement.

Behind the grocery store, in a dimly lit alleyway, Stella came to a halt, turning to face Adam with a smirk. "On your knees," she commanded, her tone leaving no room for argument.

Adam obeyed without hesitation, sinking to the ground at Stella's feet. The alleyway was dim, but the soft glow of the nearby streetlamp illuminated Stella's feet, casting an ethereal glow upon them.

Stella wiggled her toes, the polished nails catching the light as Adam's gaze remained fixated on them. "Go on," she urged, her voice a sultry whisper, "worship them."

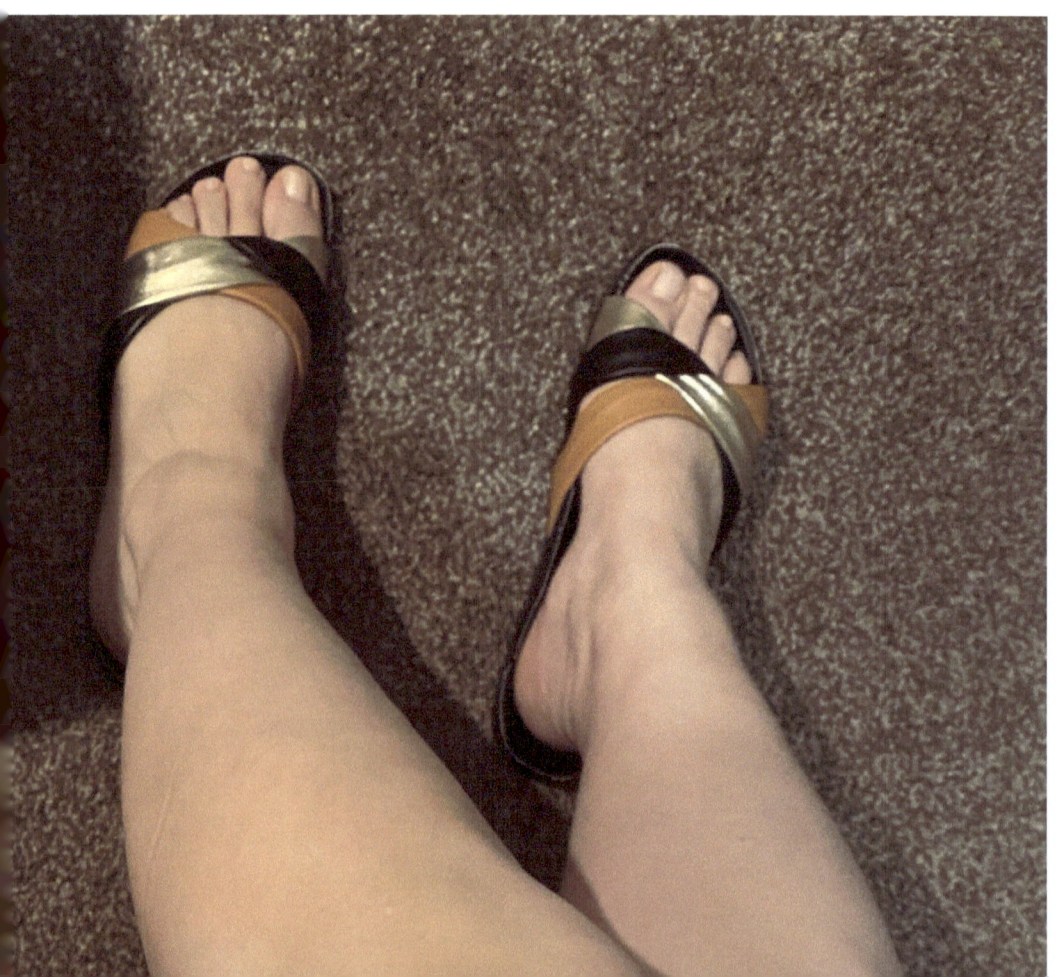

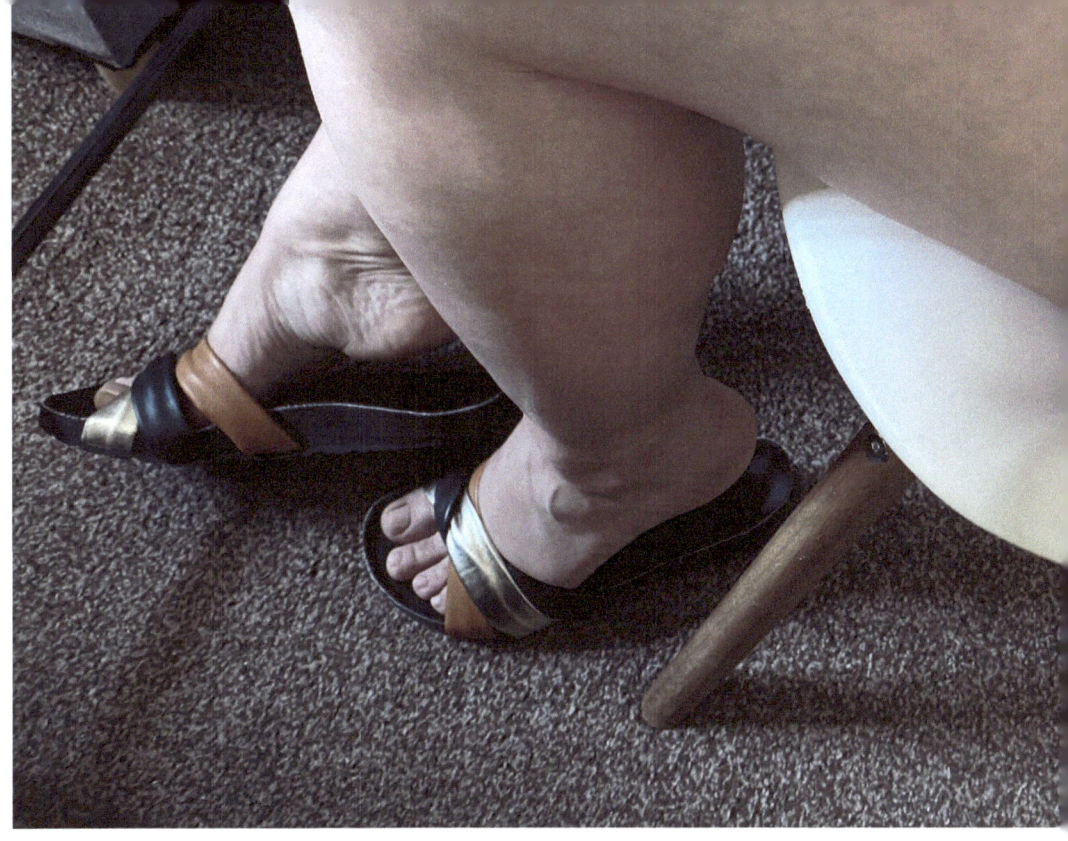

Adam hesitated for a moment, his pride warring with his desire. But as Stella's gaze bore into him, he surrendered, leaning forward to press his lips against her feet.

The smell of the alley mingled with the scent of Stella's skin, creating an intoxicating aroma that filled Adam's senses. Despite the dirt and grime beneath his knees, he found himself lost in the sensation of her soft skin against his lips.

Stella watched with amusement as Adam worshipped at her feet, his submission a testament to her power. And as he lavished attention upon her, she couldn't help but feel a sense of satisfaction—a thrill that came from knowing she held him firmly under her spell.

In that dim alleyway, amidst the discarded trash and flickering streetlights, Stella and Adam shared a moment of connection—one born from desire, dominance, and the irresistible allure of Stella's feet. And though they both knew it was forbidden, they couldn't deny the intoxicating pull that drew them together, again and again.

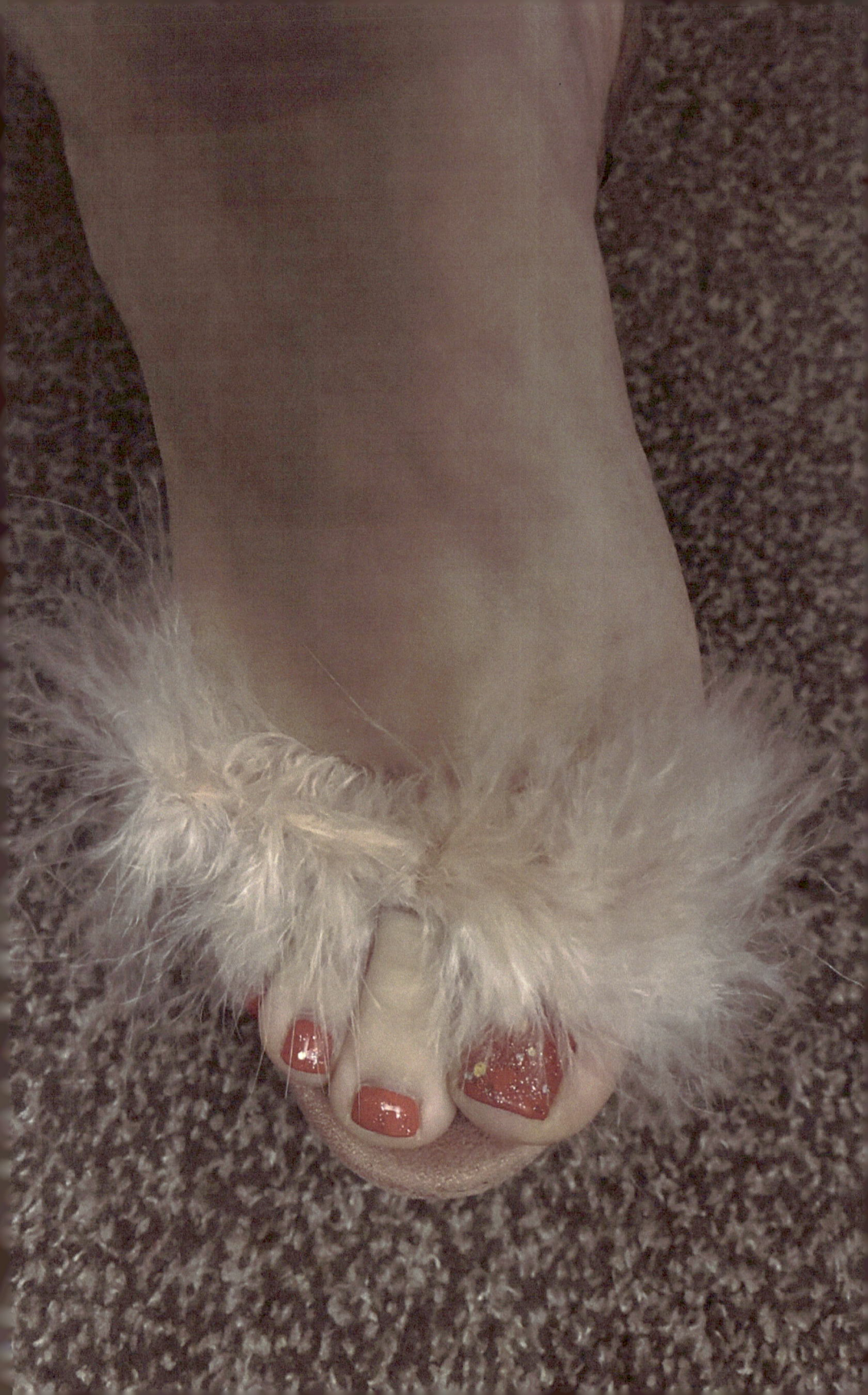

Feathered Whispers: A Tale of Intimate Encounters

I glide into the hotel room, my pulse quickening with each step. The scent of lavender envelopes me, a sweet embrace that sets the stage for our clandestine meeting. This room, our sanctuary, where the outside world fades away, leaving only us and the promise of something more.

He's already there, his eyes alight with anticipation as they meet mine. I feel a rush of warmth spread through me at the sight of him, my heart dancing to a melody only he can hear.

I pause by the door, relishing the anticipation of revealing the surprise. With a playful smile, I make my way to him, the delicate straps of my sandals securely wrapped around my ankles. Transparent and adorned with fluffy feathers, they're my most treasured possession, a whimsical touch reserved solely for him.

He gestures for me to join him on the bed, his hands reaching out to pull me close. I settle beside him, the soft duvet beneath us a comforting embrace.

"May I?" he asks, his voice a whispered plea.

I nod, a smile playing at the corners of my lips. With practised care, he gently removes my sandals, his touch sending shivers down my spine. The sensation of his fingers on my bare feet is electrifying, a reminder of the intimacy we share.

As he begins to massage and kiss my feet, I can't help but lose myself in the moment. His lips are warm against my skin, his touch tender yet possessive. It's as if every caress is a promise, a vow to cherish and protect me.

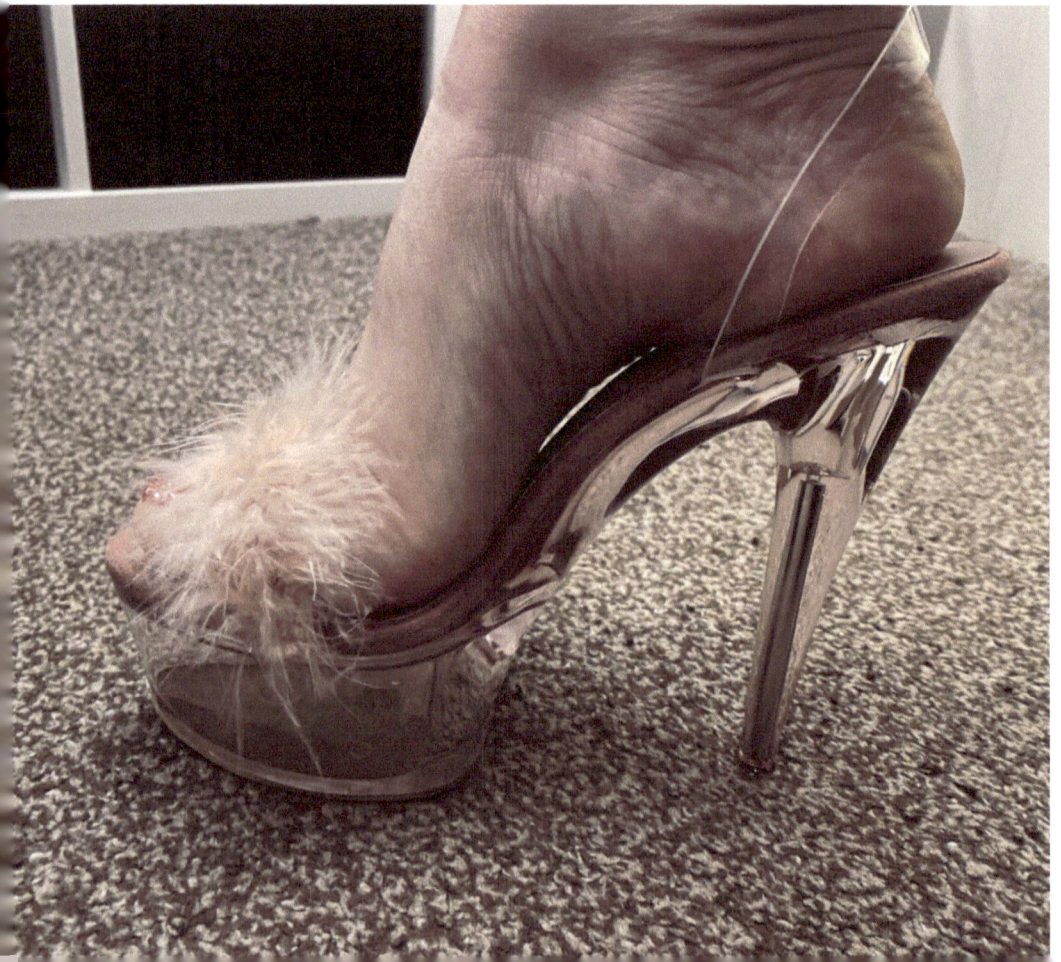

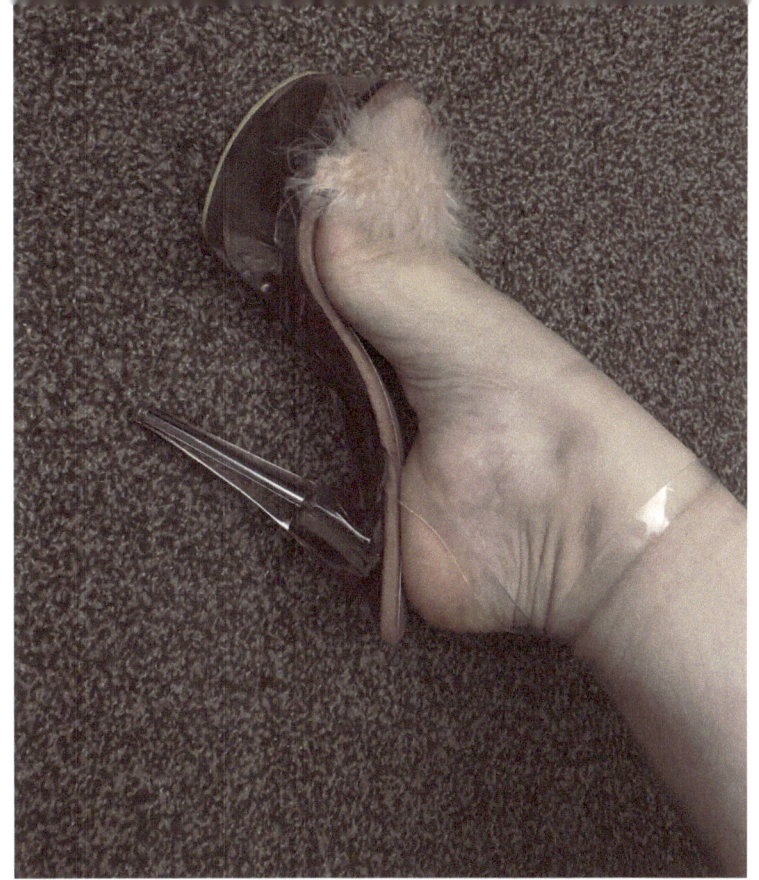

We talk as he tends to my feet, sharing secrets and dreams that we've kept hidden from the world. He tells me about his day, the challenges he faces in his work. I listen, offering words of encouragement and support.

In return, he asks about my life, curious about the woman behind the facade. I tell him about my passions, the things that make my heart sing. He listens intently, hanging onto every word as if it's the most important thing he's ever heard.

But amidst the conversation, there's an unspoken understanding between us. We both know that this is just a fleeting moment, a temporary escape from the realities of our lives. Tomorrow, we'll return to our separate worlds, each carrying a piece of the other with us.

Yet for now, we're content to live in this moment, basking in the warmth of each others presence. And as he continues to lavish attention on my feet, I can't help but feel like I'm walking on air.

Foot Stretching Routine for Flexibility and Relaxation

Embarking on my daily foot stretching routine is like stepping into a serene sanctuary, where simplicity meets efficacy. As I settle onto my mat, I begin with a deep breath, clearing my mind and setting the tone for the session ahead.

Starting with seated position, I extend my legs, grounding my feet firmly on the mat. The routine kicks off with toe curls, a simple yet effective way to awaken the muscles in my feet. I gently curl each toe, envisioning them stretching and flexing like a well-oiled machine. It's a subtle movement, but one that instantly invigorates my feet, preparing them for the stretches to come.

Moving on to the soles of my feet, I focus on flexing them, feeling the muscles along the arches and heels engage. With each flex, I sense the tension releasing, as if my feet are sighing in relief after a long day of supporting me. It's a comforting sensation, knowing that I'm giving my feet the attention they deserve.

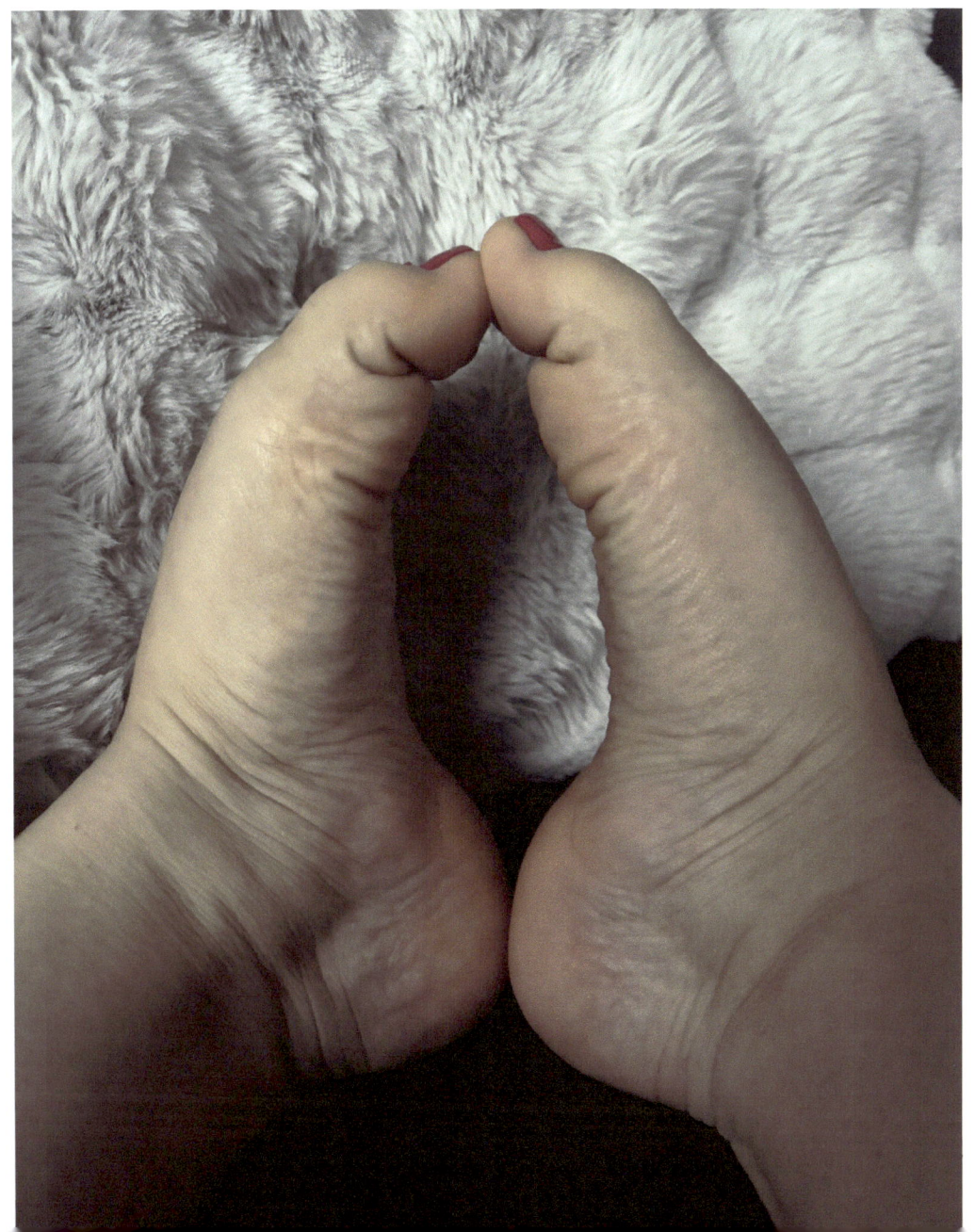

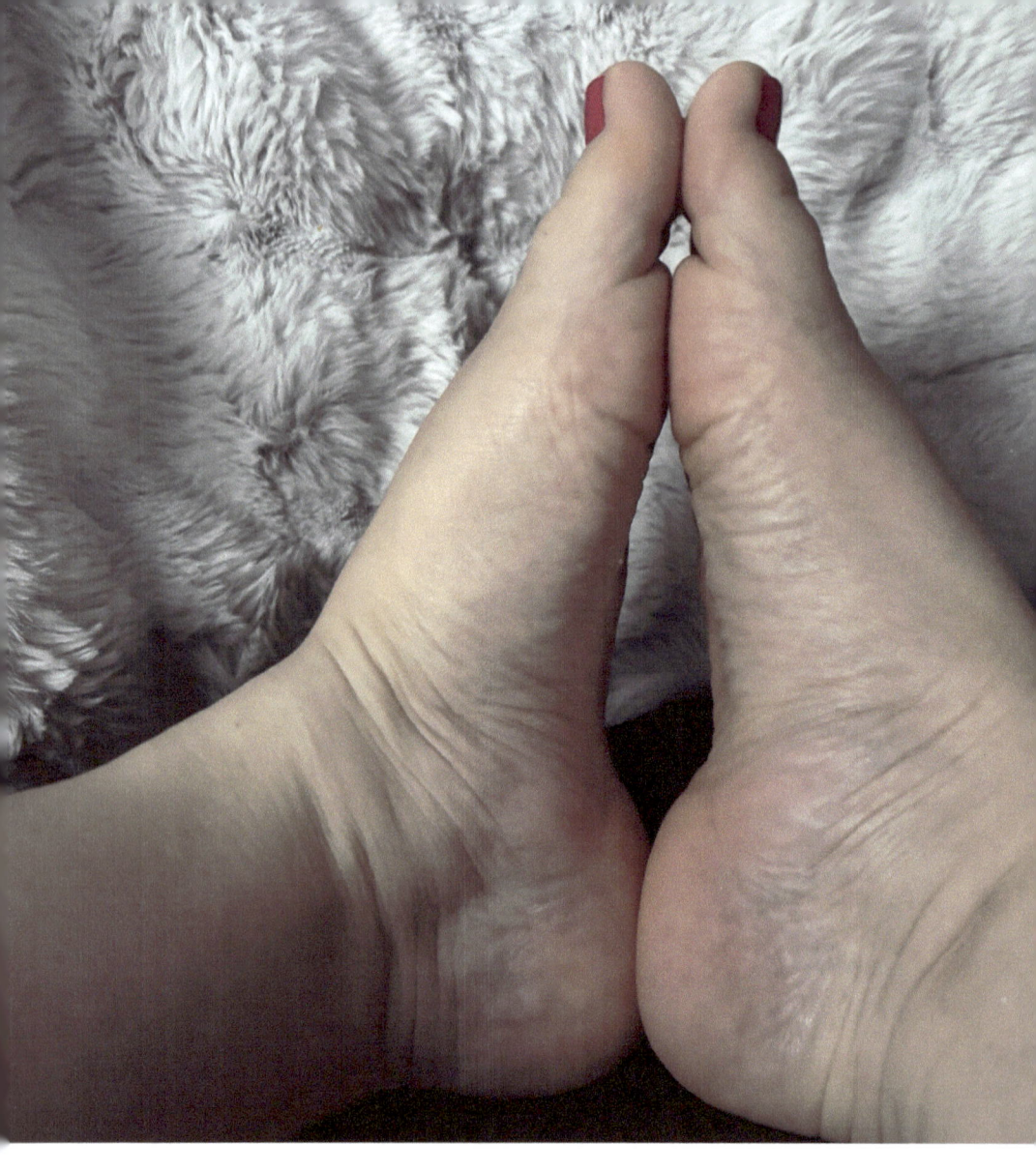

Ankle rotations come next, a fluid motion that encourages mobility and flexibility. I gently rotate my ankles in circles, feeling the joints loosen and the surrounding muscles relax. It's a simple movement, but one that has a profound impact on my overall foot health.

Throughout the routine, I maintain a sense of mindfulness, paying close attention to the sensations in my feet and how they respond to each stretch. It's a reminder to be present in the moment, to appreciate the connection between my body and mind.

By the time I finish the routine, I feel refreshed and rejuvenated, ready to tackle whatever the day may bring. And as an added bonus, my feet feel softer and more flexible, a testament to the power of regular stretching.

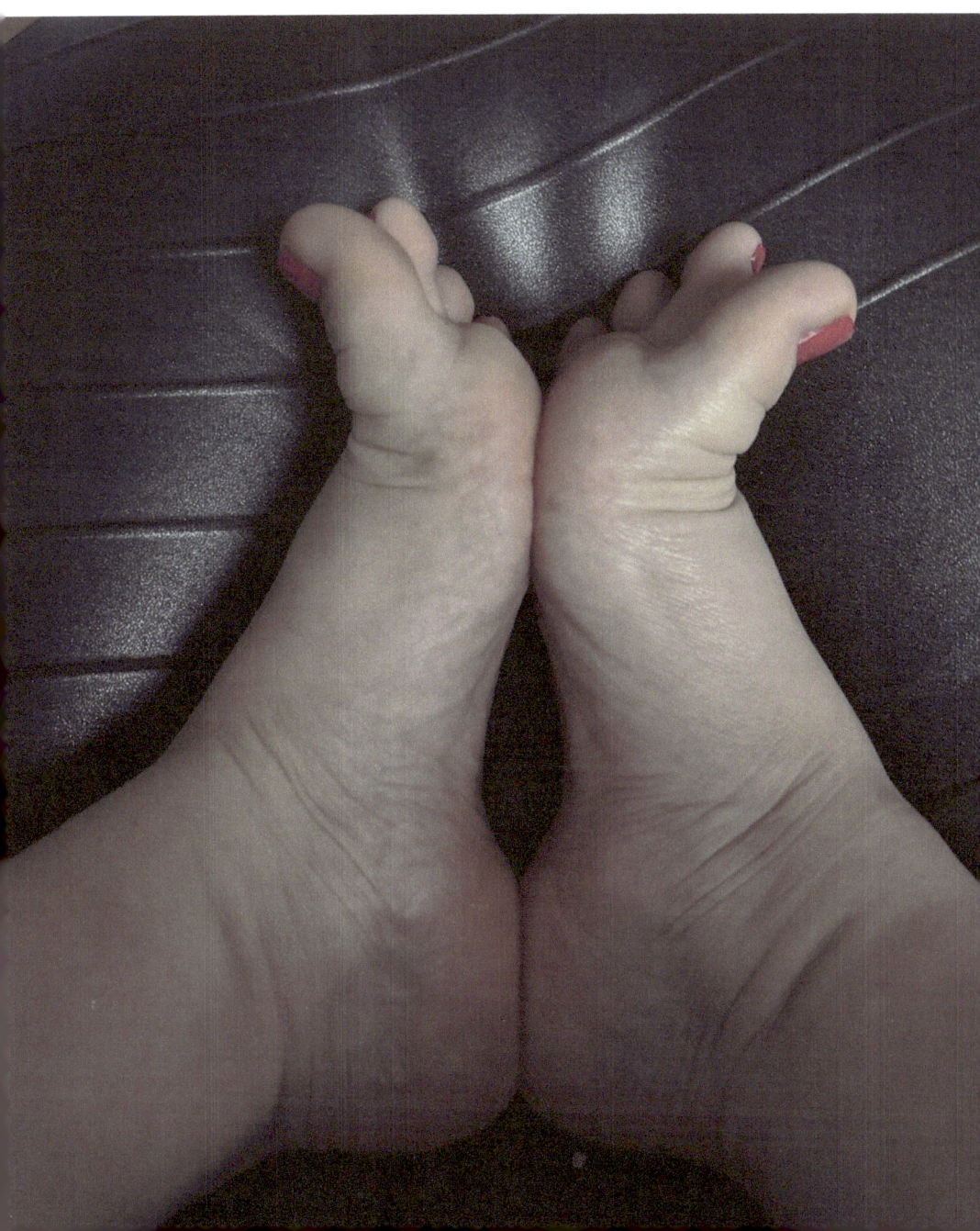

Incorporating this foot stretching routine into my daily schedule has become a ritual that I look forward to. It's a simple yet effective way to promote foot health and overall well-being, leaving me feeling grounded, relaxed, and ready to take on the world.

As I settle into my foot stretching routine, my partner often joins me, bringing warmth and support to our shared space. He enjoys watching me perform each stretch, finding joy in the little movements my toes make. His presence adds a sense of connection to the routine, turning it into a cosy moment we share together.

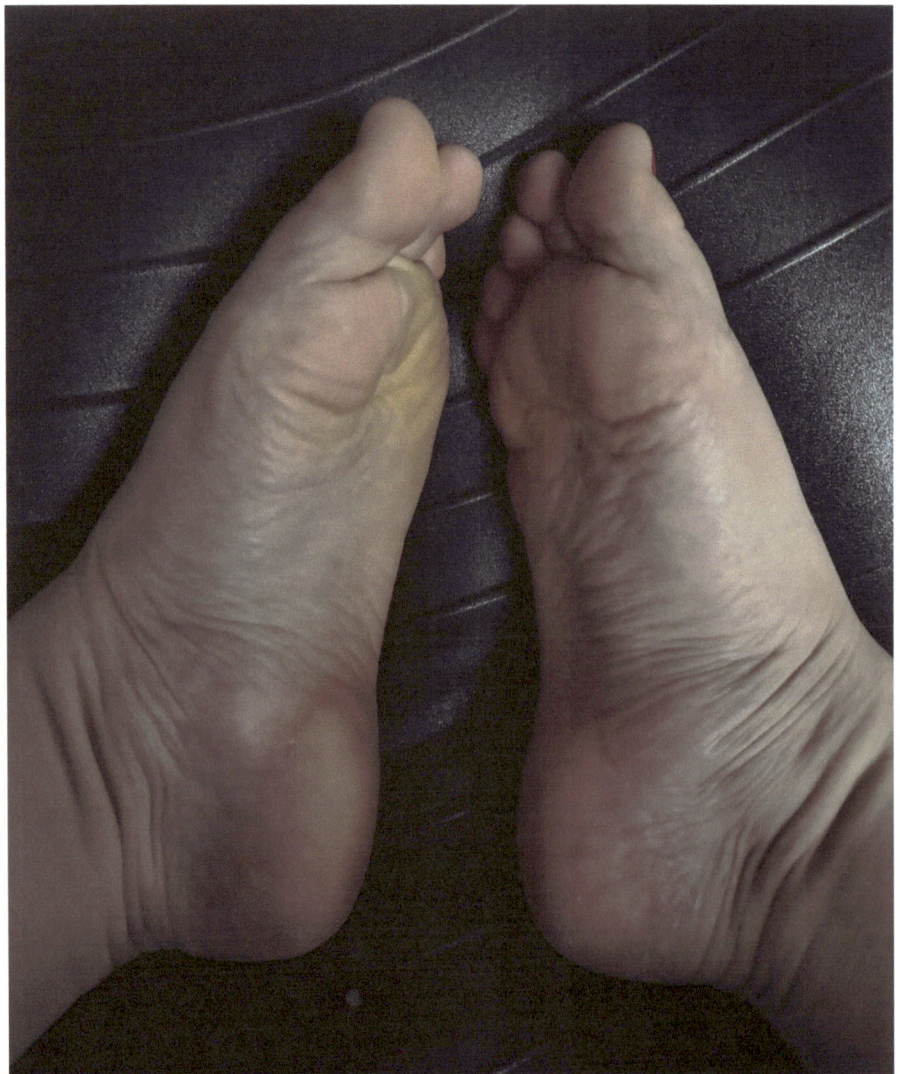

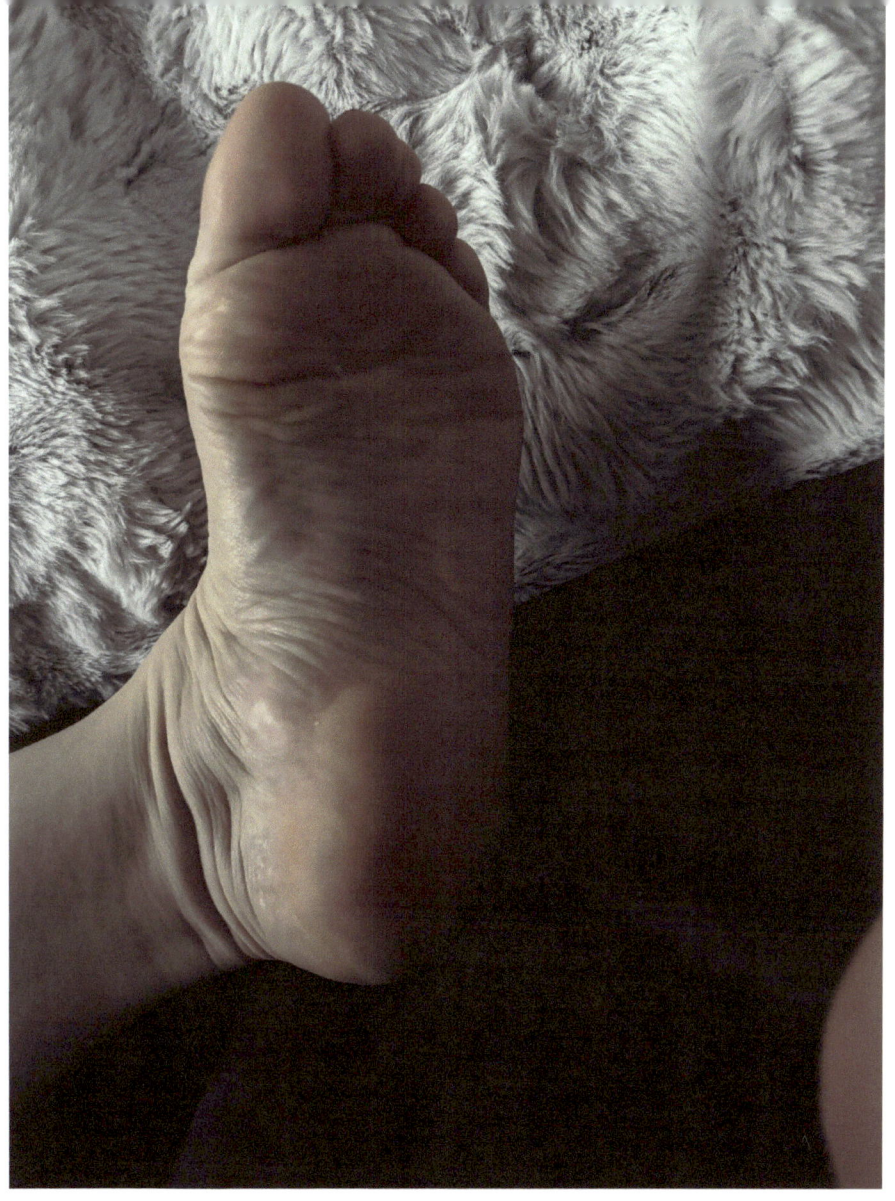

With each stretch and flex, I can feel his encouragement, his smile reflecting the pride he feels in seeing me take care of myself. He's my personal cheerleader for foot exercises, offering words of encouragement and admiration for every movement. His presence makes the routine feel lighter and more enjoyable, reminding me that self-care is not just about the physical benefits but also about the connection we share as partners.

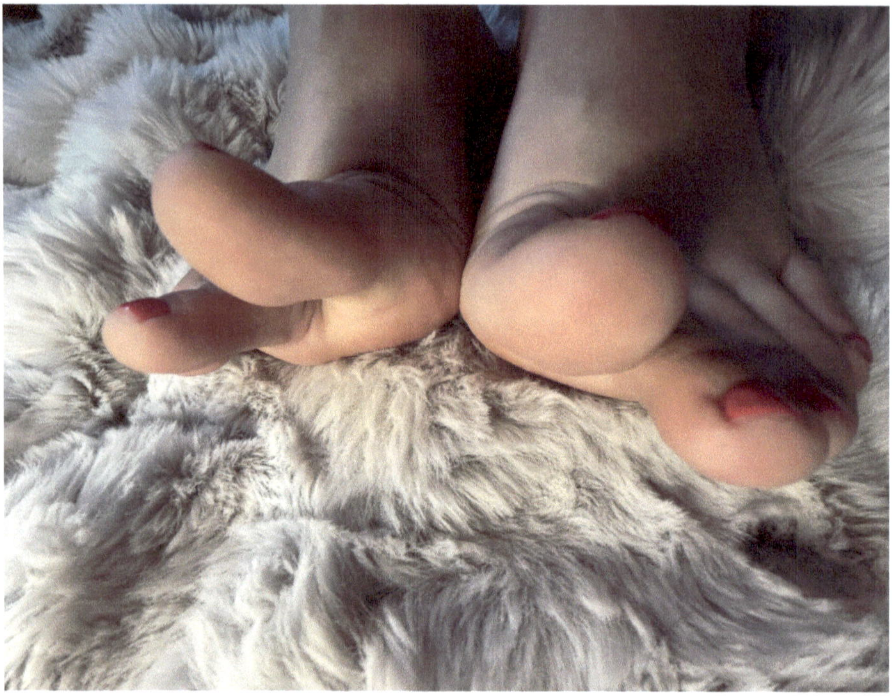

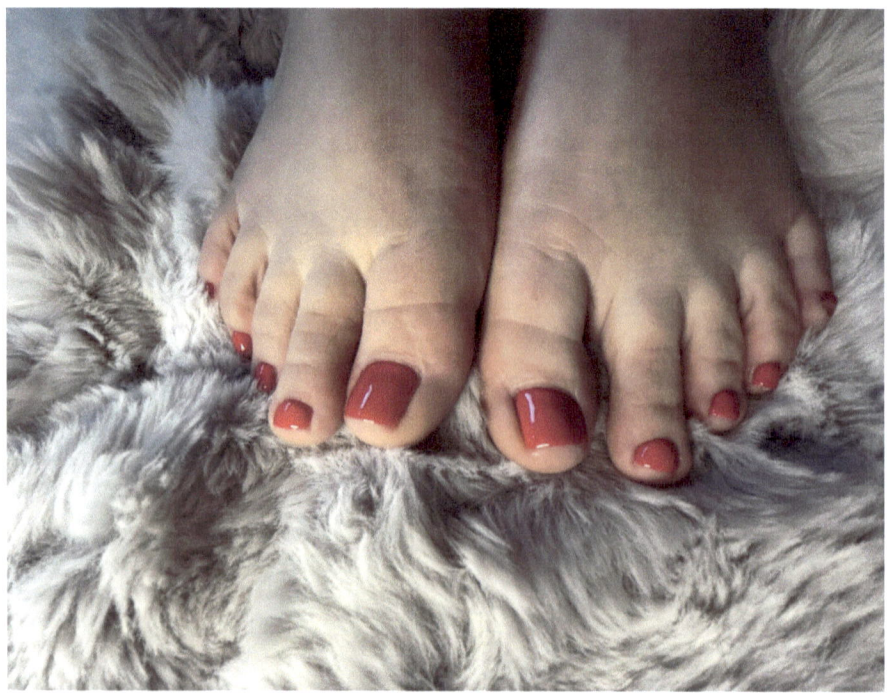

A Day of Foot Pampering and Self-Appreciation

I woke up today buzzing with excitement—it was finally my pedicure day! Skipping all the usual morning fuss, I dashed straight to the salon, eager for some much-needed pampering.

Walking into the cosy salon, I immediately felt at ease. The place smelled like a mix of fresh flowers and happiness, and I settled into the comfy chair, ready for my red-hot transformation.

The nail tech, all smiles, greeted me like an old friend. "Ready to rock your red toes, Sarah?" she said, her eyes twinkling.

Heck yeah, I was! I kicked off my shoes and sank into the chair, loving the feeling of the warm water on my feet.

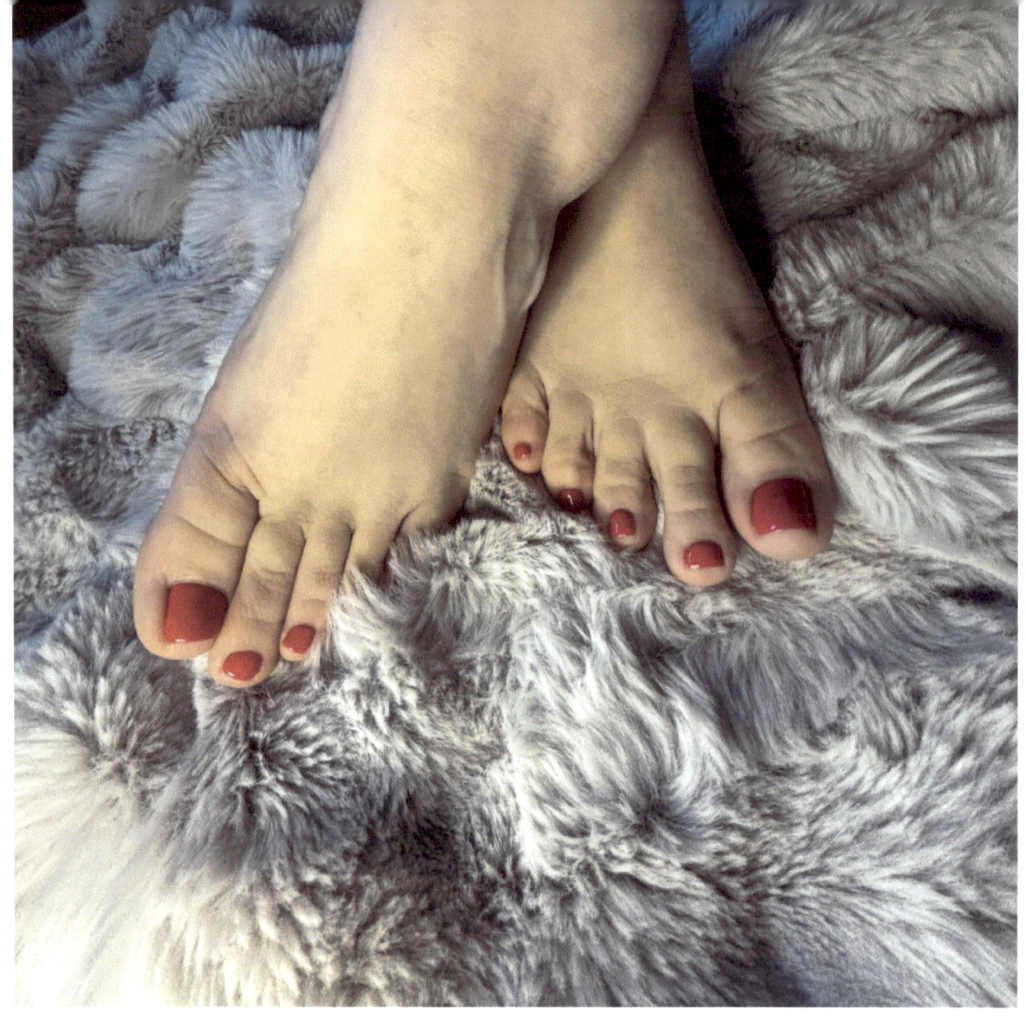

The whole pedicure was like heaven. Trimming, filing, massage—everything was on point. And when that bold red polish hit my nails, I swear I felt like a million bucks.

But the best part? The foot masks and moisturisers. My feet were never softer! I was practically purring with delight.

And of course, I couldn't resist snapping a few pics of my fancy toes. Sure, some might think it's weird, but I don't care. I love my feet, and I'm not afraid to show it!

Walking out of the salon, my feet felt lighter, and my mood was sky-high. It wasn't just about the pedicure—it was about taking some time for me, feeling good from head to toe.

And you better believe that when I strut down the street in my open-toe sandals, heads turn. Because when you feel confident and sexy, everyone else can't help but notice.

So, get this, the other day I was waiting for the bus, minding my own business, when this dude strikes up a convo with me. At first, I thought, "Cool, just a friendly chat." But then I notice his eyes keep drifting down to my feet. Like, seriously, he couldn't stop staring!

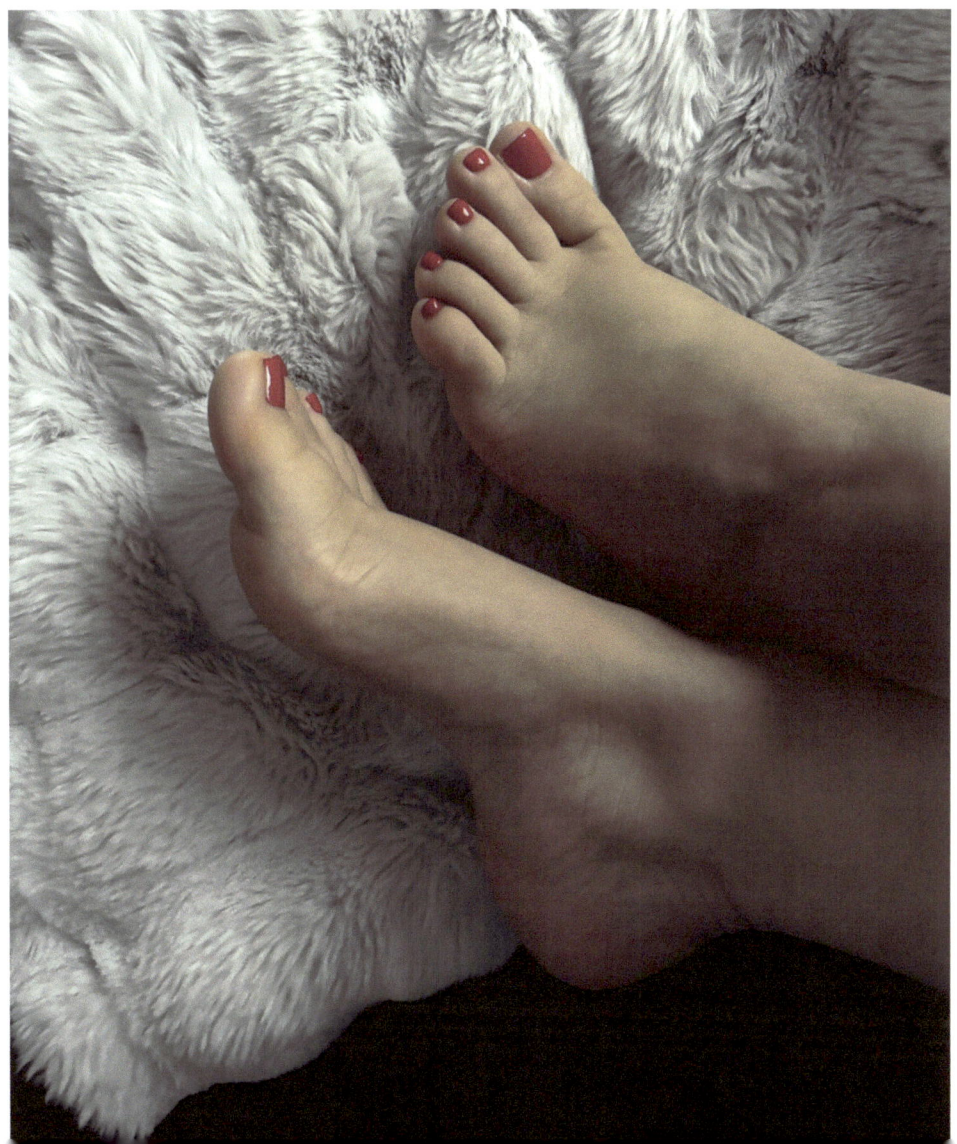

Eventually, he gathers up the guts to ask for my number, all the while sneaking peeks at my perfectly painted toes. I couldn't help but grin to myself as I handed over my digits. Who would've thought a pedicure could be such a smooth conversation starter?

Now, as I strut down the street with my freshly pampered feet peeking out of my sandals, I'm feeling like a million bucks. Sure, my flashy pedicure might turn a few heads, but hey, when you look good and feel good, why not embrace the attention? It's all part of the fun!

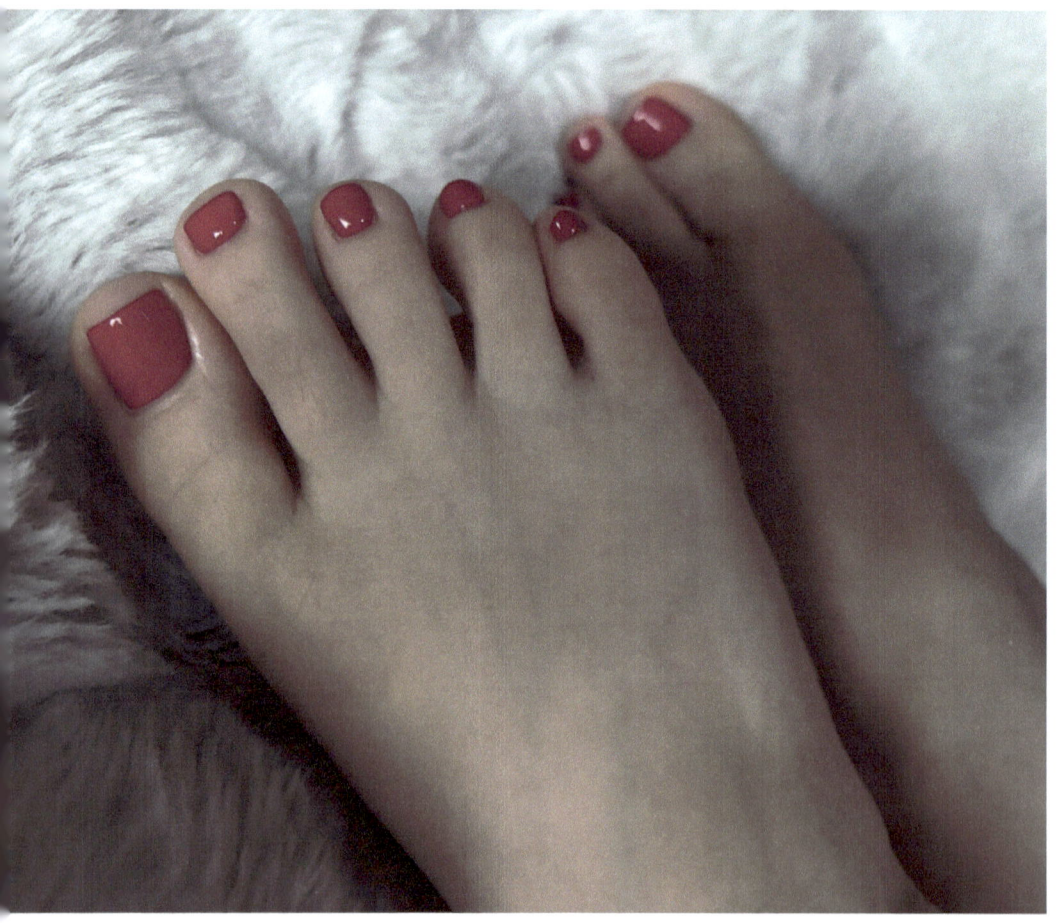

Morning Sensations

Waking up is always a slow process for me. I love the way my body stretches out after a good night's sleep, like it's waking up one limb at a time. But what really gets me going is the feeling of the bedding against my skin.

My feet are super sensitive, so every little texture is like a mini thrill. The turquoise blanket on my bed is my favourite. It's soft, but not too soft, with just the right amount of fuzziness.

As soon as I'm awake enough to move, I start playing with it. I scrunch it up with my toes, feeling the fabric bunch and fold under the pressure. It's like a little game I play with myself every morning, and it never gets old.

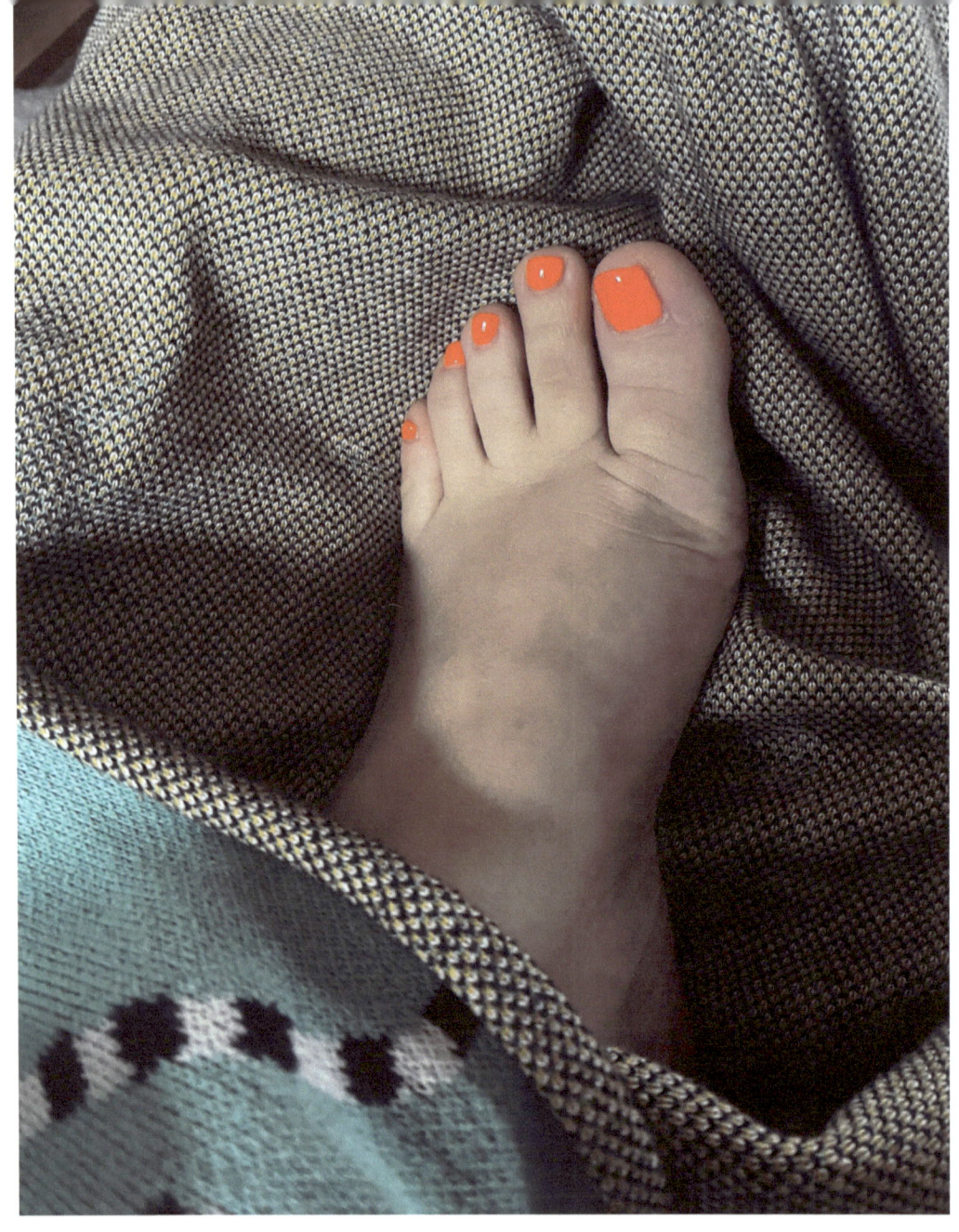

But the best part? It always gets me in the mood. There's something about the sensation of the blanket against my skin that just... does it for me. And when my partner joins in, well, let's just say things tend to escalate pretty quickly.

Before I know it, we're tangled up in each other, lost in the moment and the feeling of our bodies pressed together. It's like we're in our own little world, where nothing else matters except for the here and now.

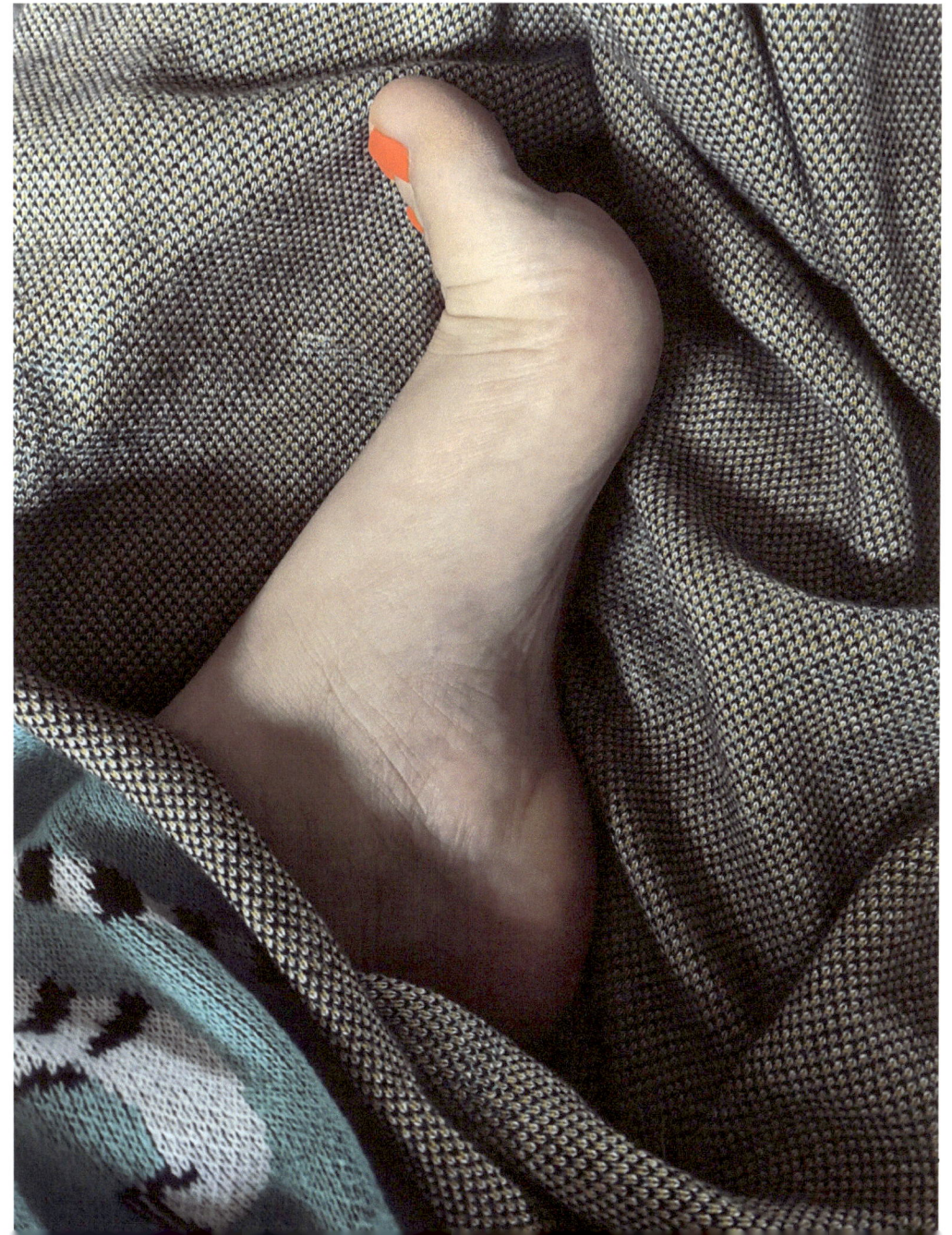

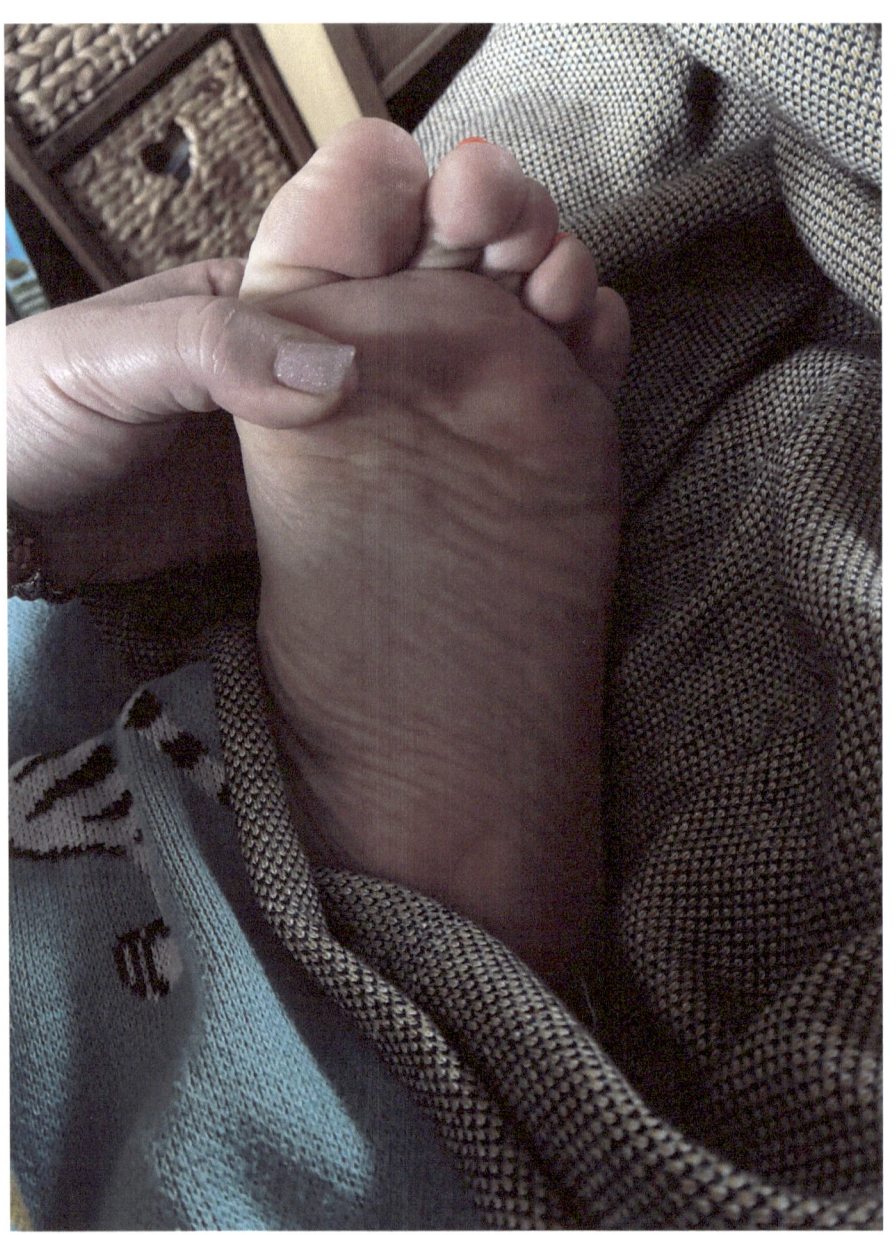

And when it's all said and done, and we're lying there in the aftermath, I can't help but smile. Because even though it started with something as simple as playing with a blanket, it always ends with us feeling closer than ever.

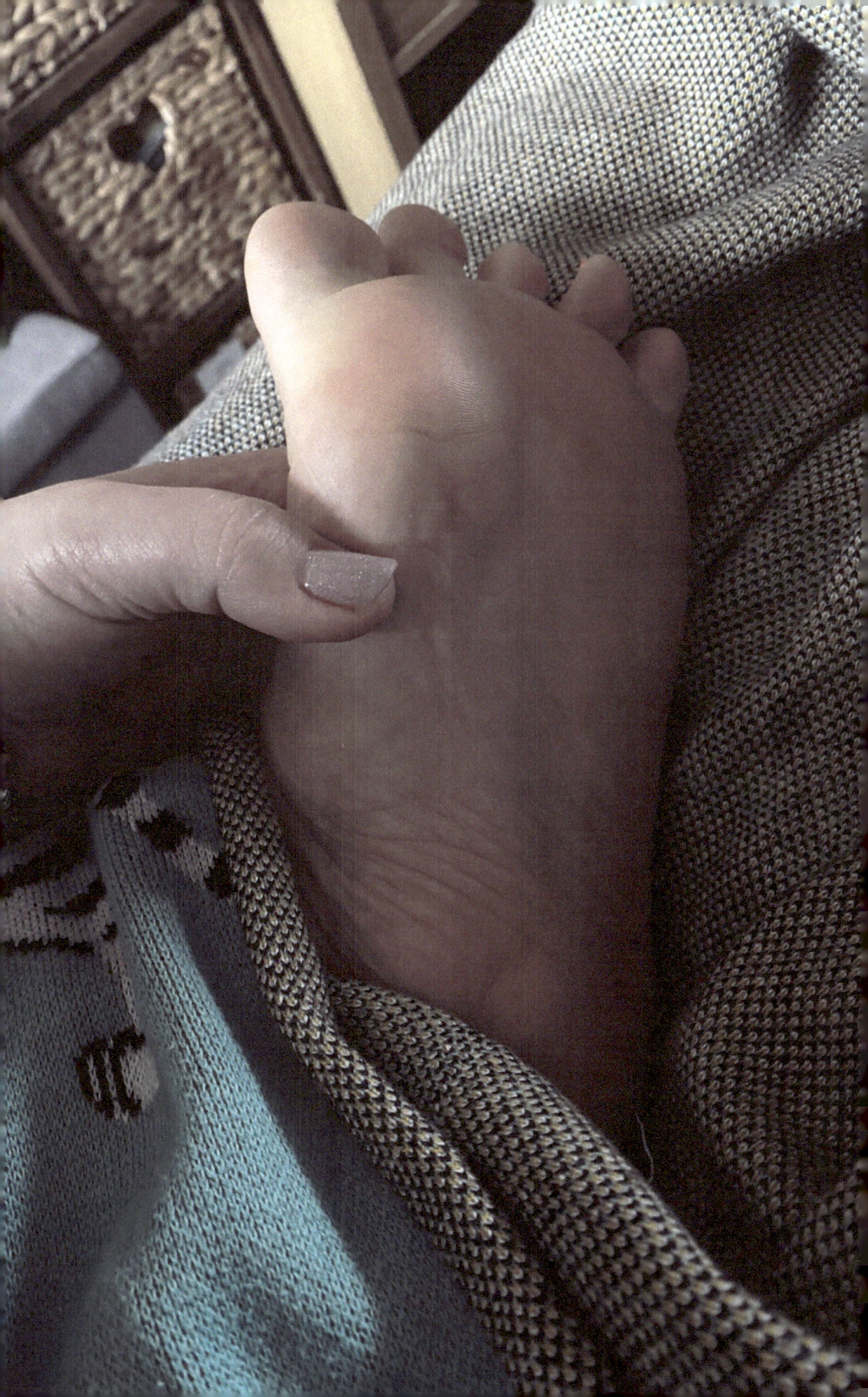

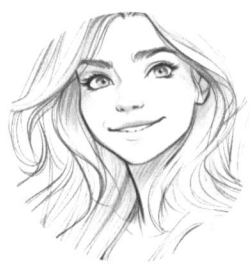

About the Author

Luna Wylde is a young female in England who has spent her time investigating the sexual desires of men and adult entertainment. Luna's captivation with foot fetishism has led her to produce spellbinding content that now includes stories written alongside alluring pictures of her feet.

In these narratives, she takes readers into a mesmerising world where imagination meets erotica thus appealing to their five senses at once. You can either get in touch with Luna via her website or wait for more exciting books about her feet adventures. Passion, creativity and exploration of dreams through words and images are what drive wild works by Luna.